Raising Teens In A Contrary Culture

MARK GREGSTON

FIRST EDITION

ISBN: 978-1-946466-48-8

Library of Congress Control Number: 2018952696

Published by

Certa
PUBLISHING

P.O. Box 2839, Apopka, FL 32704

In partnership with

heartlight
publishing

Printed in the United States of America

Table of Contents

Dedication

This book is dedicated to Stitch, a dear friend that has set at my feet day and night as I have pecked out the words of this book and all my other pennings. A four-legged, important part of our family, Stitch, takes care of my wife, Jan, while I'm on the road. Stitch is that silent presence in our home that has taught me the value of listening. I'm convinced that if I could be half the person she thinks I am, I would be twice the man that I am today.

Acknowledgments

A special thanks to the Heartlight Foundation Board of Directors for their never-ending commitment to give guidance and direction to the development of new ways to help more and more families across North America.

And, thank you to Heartlight's Board of Directors who oversee the operation of the Heartlight residential program and help provide a wonderful respite of help and hope for so many families caught in crisis.

Serving on the board for years was a dear friend, Bill O'Connell, who helped guide and direct Heartlight as it entered its "teen years." Rest in peace, my dear friend…your life affected the lives of many.

To all our donors and supporters who have invested in the growth of Heartlight over the last thirty years, I am most thankful. You have played a major part in creating options and opportunities for families who are changing their future.

To our radio team of Roger Kemp & Company, I am most grateful. Who would have thought that a few trials at Mole's End would create a program that is heard around the world?

A special thanks to our marketing team of C2 Media in Nashville, the Next After group from Dallas, and Mike Blanton of Blanton Entertainment, all who continue to help us reach more and more parents and teens.

And a shout out to Doug Kindy and Randy Steele of Lucchese Boots who make sure that my legacy of footwear continues.

Words can never express the amount of appreciation that I have for our Heartlight staff who work tirelessly to provide a haven of hope and a place of help for all the teens who live with us on the Heartlight campus. These guys and gals do the heavy lifting and change the destiny of families on a daily basis.

I so appreciate the opportunity to work with all the staff of the Heartlight Foundation who tolerates my busy schedule and keeps us looking good in the eyes of those needing help.

I am blessed to be able to work with my family. Their involvement at Heartlight makes it a joy to get up every day and work together, to offer help and hope to parents and teens in a broken world.

And last, but certainly not least, I am grateful to Jan, my wife of forty-three years, who has been instrumental in every aspect of our ministry together. Who would have thought that the first date to a Led Zeppelin concert in Tulsa would one day have us doing what we do forty-nine years later?

Introduction

I'm sure you're a lot like me when I say that I'm glad I don't have to be raised in the culture our teens have to grow up in. It's different than what you and I experienced, and chances are, it's unlike what we experienced even a few years ago with other kids that have passed through our home.

Being different doesn't mean that it's all bad—it's just different. The problem with this difference is when the parenting styles and tools that you and I possessed and used with other kids don't work with the ones currently living with us. So, even what you're doing that isn't working isn't wrong, it may just mean that you need to try something different to get a different result from your child.

It's my hope that you'll gain some insight from this book, insight that lends a different perspective and a practical approach for your parenting intentions. Maybe it will mean learning a new parenting skill, or discovering a new way of communicating, or gaining an understanding of a facet of the adolescent culture affecting your teen. It's a different culture that is going to demand a different method if you're going to impact the way your teen reacts to a contrary culture or responds to your attempts to maintain that connection you've worked years to build.

I hope you enjoy this book as much as I've enjoyed writing it. It's based on just about all the wit and wisdom I've collected over the past forty years and through the thousands of teens who have lived with us at Heartlight. Because of the trust of the same number of families who have leaned on our expertise at Heartlight to give spiritual insight and practical application to the challenges faced by moms and dads throughout the years, I share these time-tested concepts with you with the intent of helping you remain connected to your teens throughout their adolescent years.

Mark Gregston

CHAPTER 1

Challenges Facing Parents of Teens

*I urge you, brothers and sisters, to watch out for those who cause divisions and put obstacles in your way that are **contrary** to the teaching you have learned.*

Romans 16:17

Do you know any parent that was excited to find out that the relationship with their teen was conflictive, contradictory, oppositional, and irreconcilable? No parent that I've ever met! But it happens all the time. Many parents, who once had a great connection with their child, find their relationship is becoming strained during the adolescent years. They begin to wonder what happened to the dreams, hopes, and longings for the good things desired for that young daughter or son, as they handed coffee mugs and T-shirts that screamed *World's Greatest Dad* or *World's Greatest Mom*.

Who would have ever believed something that had been good for so many years, could become so distant and detached, especially after all those years of coaching soccer, baseball, ice hockey, or after years of pouring your life into your child as a mom or dad?

It's hard to believe, and even harder to imagine, how something that was once so good could have the possibility of going so bad, but it can. And if you find yourself in that situation, chances are the feelings of hope and connection with your teen left your expectations long ago. What parent would have ever thought this to be possible?

I believe many overestimate the effectiveness of their parenting skills and grossly underestimate how the effect of today's culture is changing the nature of their relationship with their adolescent children. And they wonder, "How could something that had been going so well, turn so bad, so quickly?"

Many overestimate the effectiveness of their parenting skills and grossly underestimate the effect of today's culture.

The answer is easy. It's caused by the contrary culture that our teens are living in.

Kids hit the middle school years, and the slow but ever-moving wave of change begins to come ashore in the lives of families. It's the groundswell beginnings of adolescence that thrust your innocent pre-teen into a world of exposure, new communication, social upheaval, negative influence, and false maturity that convinces teens they can handle much more than they are capable.

Parents begin to ask questions never asked before, struggling to find answers to counter the effects of a contrary culture; a world of opposing viewpoints and opinions that tend to gently sway a young teen's heart to find attraction to concepts, lifestyles, and attitudes that are completely "on the other side" of how they've been raised.

They find themselves asking:

"What are we supposed to do?"
"How do I counter the effects and presence of this culture on my teen?"
"How do we recognize potential problems?"
"Why does my child do what he or she does?"

"How can my child violate all that we're about?"

"Why do I feel like my parenting skills are no longer effective?"

"I try to connect with me teen; why is nothing working?"

Have these questions ever bounced around in your heart as you've watched your sweet little girl mature into a young lady, or your little boy transform into a questioning smart aleck who challenges everything all the time?

The culture is a little different than when you and I grew up, isn't it?

Here are just a few things that have changed, and they're just the tip of the iceberg.

- Marijuana is legalized in many states now.
- Gender issues dominate the media.
- Teens communicate more with their fingers than with their voices.
- 4.3 million porn sites demand supervision on the Internet.
- More pictures are taken every two seconds than were taken in all of the 1800s.
- Teens spend an average of ten hours a day looking at some type of screen.
- Entitlement prevails.
- There's little respect for authority.
- Adolescents spend most of their time in the shallow end of the relationship pool.
- Masses of kids are leaving the church upon graduation from high school.
- Everyone is encouraged to speak his/her thoughts, with platforms to do so.
- The American Medical Association has increased the age of adolescence to age twenty-seven.
- Our teens live in an appearance and performance world.

- Forty-two percent of girls and forty-six percent of guys, between the ages of fifteen and seventeen, have engaged in oral sex in the last six months.
- The court of public opinion seems to "trump" due process.
- Little is left to the imagination.
- Bullying dominates the news, and teens spend more time recording conflicts, rather than engaging in resolution.
- Mass school shootings appear to be more prevalent.

A little different than the world you and I grew up in, isn't it?

Parents are frustrated that the parenting tools they've used so effectively in their child's earlier years are no longer working with the same results. Our teens live in a world of high anxiety and deep frustration, with hints of anger and depression visiting homes dedicated to wanting God's best for their children. It's a world that you and I have said we're glad we don't have to grow up in.

It's a contrary culture, not always working with us but seemingly operating against us most of the time. Now, I'm not one of those guys who hates the world, but I sure understand the influence and impact the culture is having on parents who desire to raise a godly family.

Don't give up. Hope is not lost!

The role parents (and grandparents) have in today's culture is to maintain a household of love, preserving the rules and boundaries that help keep a child on the *right* path, while encouraging independence and responsibility. This creates a place of rest from the craziness of a culture that never rests. Just as you feel the "pinch" of your values being challenged in a permissive culture, I can guarantee you, your child feels the same, if not worse.

And since they are the ones that have to live in it, the responsibility lies on you, the parent, to provide a haven of rest and a place of respite from a culture that is attacking the heart of your teen. When Jesus says, *"Come to me all who are weary and heavy laden, and I will give you REST"* (Matthew 11:28). He's giving an example of one who can "keep their cool" while challenged by the world of influence.

However, many times we're just as busy as our kids, and we forget their world is more confusing and conflictive to them than it is to any parent. It's easy to armchair quarterback our child's life from a distance, but it's another thing to actually be on the playing field, taking the hits and tackles, which sometimes stop or injure the players (your teens) and causes them to stumble.

I don't know about you, but I find that many times, in my busyness, I forget what is most valuable in my pursuit of what I think is more important. Jan, my wife of forty-three years, and I were headed to Cabo San Lucas, Mexico for a break in the craziness of my busy schedule, which I am sure is no busier than yours. We pulled up at 4:30 p.m. to our little airport in Longview, Texas, where there are two flights a day, and we both got out of my truck in front of

I find that many times, in my busyness, I forget what is most valuable in my pursuit of what I think is more important.

the ticket counter to go in and check-in our luggage. (It's a small airport—really small!)

Jan (who sometimes feels like she needs to take everything she owns on a short vacation) had too many bags, most of which were overweight and subject to restrictions on flying. As we discussed the poundage, she wanted to get on the plane. My focus zeroed in on getting through security and getting on the plane so we could get to our next destination. We left Longview and arrived in Dallas, only to find out that our flight to Cabo was delayed. Four hours later, we got on our next flight, at midnight. The second I stepped onto the plane I remembered something...

I left my truck running out in front of the airport, eight hours ago!

In pursuit of something that I *thought* was important, I forgot what just might be more valuable. Ever feel that way when you see your teen struggle a bit—like maybe you forgot to pay attention to that child who desperately needs you while you're pursuing what you *think* is important? It's easy to do. I do it all the time. It's when we see our kids stumble that we look at our priorities. I can tell you this: They need you now! So, don't pursue the seemingly *important* and neglect the *valuable*.

Here are a couple of things that I would say to any parent:

First, if you have pre-teens, get prepared for the upcoming adolescent years. Don't lean on your own understanding, believing what worked in the past will continue to work in the future. What I mean is this: The parenting skills that were rewarded with special coffee mugs and T-shirts, won't work during the teen years. Don't fool yourself, because you can't fool your child. If you rely on what worked in the past, you won't enjoy the days ahead in the future.

Second, if you're going through a struggle with your teen, then look at this series as a way to lighten up a bit, and learn to do some different things. Simply put, what was once effective won't be soon. And what worked in the past, won't work in the future. It's not that you don't possess good parenting skills, because you do. But you might just need to add a few more tools to your parenting toolbox to have the right ones for the teen years.

I share my insights with a couple of assumptions, which I hope you'll embrace.

Dads, I will never tell you that you are wrong. (Men don't like that, do they?) But I will suggest other ways that may be more effective for engaging your teen son or daughter.

Mom, no one cares about your kids more than you. However, that caring can sometimes keep your child from growing up. You're not wrong, and can never be, in loving your teen, but the timing of how you show your care could be a bigger issue than you think. And to you, grandparent, teens need your wisdom and involvement. Don't think God is keeping you alive longer so that you'll play more shuffleboard. He will use you to give your grandkids something they can't get anywhere else.

Your teens need you more than ever! *You* are God's answer to a crazy culture, which isn't helping the parenting process very much. I'm convinced that the way you handle your kids during the teen years, regardless of how things went during their younger years, will determine the type of relationship you will have with your child in the coming decades.

CHAPTER 2

The Importance of Your Parenting Role

Each day of our lives we make deposits in the memory banks of our children.

Charles R. Swindoll

The previous chapter discussed the current condition of the culture and the effect it's having on our teens, and how we should consider changing our parenting style to more effectively "fit" the needs of our teens. As I mentioned earlier, if you hold on to the parenting style that worked during your child's preteen years—at a period where their social world is changing rapidly—it won't work.

I promise you this: What you do during your child's adolescent years will make all the difference in the world in what your family will look like once your child leaves your home (and also when they bring their own kids back home to visit you). Your relationship with your child is of utmost importance. Without it, your child's future wedding (whether it be four or fourteen years from now) will be just a little more than a celebration of regret. Your involvement in the life of your adult children will be minimal, and your influence and legacy on your kids and grandkids will be non-existent.

I've always told folks this: The healthiness and ongoing welfare of your family will be consumed in three important areas of focus. Constant attention and faithful pursuit of balancing these areas of your home will

provide a greater chance of having a healthy home life. On the opposite side, the neglect of these areas will only confuse and damage your relationship with your teen.

What you do during your child's adolescent years will make all the difference in the world in what your family will look like once your child leaves your home.

Here are the three most important areas of your teen's life that will demand your attention and require your participation so that your relationship with them will continue to flourish once they leave home and begin a life on their own.

Relational Atmosphere

The first one is the *relational atmosphere* of your home. If you listen to me on the radio, read my articles, hear me speak, or spend any time with me at all, you'll know that I believe the relationship you have with your child is of utmost importance. It is the relationship that will continue to speak to them when they are lost. It's the relationship that will speak truth into their life when they're following falsehoods. It's your relationship that will affirm life when they feel anything but good in life. It is your relationship with them that will speak to them of worth when they feel worthless, and it's your relationship that will usher in hope when they feel hopeless. It's important to retain that relationship no matter what choices they make or what direction their life takes, as in a movement toward or totally away from the Lord. The key to a relationship is to love unconditionally, to affirm their existence at their worst of times, and to let them know they are loved when they feel unlovable.

The bottom line is this: Your relationship with your children is important!

Here's the kicker. There's only one person in this world you can change and that is *you*. Some parents think they can change their kids. I silently snicker as I write this because I'm convinced, after years of living with over thousands of teens, that I can't really change any of them. I can only provide the atmosphere of change and a relationship of unconditional love. They have to be the ones who decide to change. So, if you're the only person you can change, then it's essential that you strive to make the changes that will continue to keep your relationship with your teen engaging.

With that being said, how do you relate to your teen? How do you engage with your family? Are you a stick in the mud or are you one who laughs and enjoys life? Do you share experiences with others, not only in words, but in participation with others? Is there something you are doing that is pushing your teen away from you? If you can't answer that question, then text them the question now. Ask them if you're doing something that is pushing them away. Ask them if they think you are doing something that is getting in the way of your relationship growing deeper.

It's important to retain that relationship with your teen, no matter what choices they make.

And here's the hardest part. If they tell you that you're doing something that is causing division, just listen. Don't share your opinion, and don't invalidate or undermine their response. Just listen. Let their comments set in for a couple of days and spend some time thinking about how to respond. Instead of looking at all the "specks" in their life, look at the possibility that there might be a "log" in your own eye. What is amazing about all of this is that sometimes we, as normal human beings, can't even see a log in our eye—a log that may be distorting our vision and blurring what is meant to be seen clearly. That's an interesting thought, isn't it? Perhaps the reason there is conflict in your home is you're not seeing what needs to be noticed because of your unwillingness to remove what is blinding your vision of what truly needs to be seen.

The goal is to create an atmosphere where your teen can share all that you are doing which is keeping the relationship from growing. It's not a time to argue who is right and who is wrong. It's a time to figure out *why*—regardless of the reason—the relationship isn't working and what you can do to change the outcome of what your family will look like in the days ahead.

Structure of Your Home

The second area of your teen's life is how you structure your home, how you set expectations, and how you strategize your rules and consequences. At some point, kids no longer accept your rules just because you stated them (usually at the beginning of their teen years). That's when you'll have to strategize and outline your expectations, determine the boundaries, and set rules to keep them on the path of pursuing what they determine to be good for their life.

Discipline is helping a child get to where they want to go, and keeping them from ending up where they never want to be. It's all about them. The parenting shift that begins to happen is one which lets them know the rules are not about fulfilling what Mom and Dad desire, but they are designed to help them get what they want and keep them away from what they don't want.

Discipline is helping a child get to where they want to go, and keeping them from ending up where they never want to be.

In reality, the rules that worked the first twelve years of your child's life were about you. Those rules defined what you desired for them and what you expected from them. The focus of the rules must begin to shift during the adolescent years so that your upcoming teens will realize the rules are about helping them get where they want to go.

All rules should encourage the positive behavior and serve up consequences for poor choices that would take them off the course they want to achieve. Please hear me on this particular point. Surely, if your son decides he wants to be a marijuana dealer, a parent doesn't allow or support behavior that can ultimately destroy his life. A parent should never encourage or reinforce a negative or potentially damaging behavior.

All rules should be set up to provide a reward if followed, and a defined consequence that is strong and painful enough to keep a teen from making a contrary choice to the rule. Remember, your teen will continue the inappropriate behavior until the pain of their actions is greater than the pleasure they get from their behavior.

When developing rules for your home, limit the number of rules to be kept to under ten, and don't exasperate your teen with "150 rules of operation." That would only provoke them to frustration. Ask the following questions for each rule:

- Is there a clear definition of what is allowed and what is not?
- What are the consequences that would keep my teen from continuing the negative and inappropriate behavior?
- Are the rules age-appropriate, effective, and purposeful?
- Do the rules transfer choices to your child, where they also understand the consequences?

Your rules should define what you and your home will be about and what your home will not be. Make no mistake; your teen wants structure. And, believe it or not, they really want rules to follow. If you have a difficult time determining rules and consequences, I have written a workbook called *Developing Rules & Consequences* that can help you come up with rules for your home.

Deal with the True Issues

The third area of your teen's life is their *heart*. You can have a great relationship with your teen, and have the finest set of rules in place, but if you don't deal with the critical and deeper issues of the heart, you will only be postponing resolution to a later date. At that time, the results of unresolved issues will affect even more people and have greater consequences. You must deal with the issues of the heart. If not, you will just be managing behavior instead of changing the true motivation for the behavior.

Deal with the heart issues. So, with all that in mind, ask yourself some questions.

- What's really motivating my child's behavior?
- What are some of the issues that have been ignored or just missed?
- Does there need to be counseling involved for the healthiness of my child?
- Is medication to help with anxiety, depression, or a mood disorder necessary? Is there a need for medical intervention?
- Is there a heart issue that needs to be focused on through a little probing and discussion?

As I said earlier, if you don't spend time getting to the *heart issues*, you are merely spending more time controlling your teen's behavior under the false presumption that your relationship with your son or daughter is just fine. The visible behavior you see is a reflection of the invisible, and oftentimes, the unresolved issues in the life of your teen. Create an environment that puts relationships first, structured to help your teen grow and mature while getting to the heart of the issues that arise during the teen years.

Shift Your Parenting Style

Teens want to be prepared to live in the world they are going to live in, not the one that *you* hope they'll live. You can either raise your kids to live in a zoo, or you can prepare them to survive in the jungle. I think your teen desires the latter. Stated as simply as I can, when your children enter their teen years, you must switch your model of influence from teaching to training. To explain what I mean, let me break it down into a list of what you must move away from and move toward.

Move from Allowing Immaturity to Encouraging Maturity

Twelve-year-olds are expected to be immature because they are. When they turn thirteen, it's important that everyone involved in the life of the child, including grandparents, begin the push toward maturity. Even in a grandparent's home, it should not be a place where a young thirteen- to fourteen-year-old can retreat and escape the growing-up process. That would be in direct conflict with the desires of the parents.

No one wants to have a twenty-five-year-old lounge lizard hanging out on the sofa, playing video games, with no job, no drive, and no direction in life. Hopefully, you didn't allow them to do that. Once they enter the teen years, it's time to start growing up. Encouraging maturity includes, but is not limited to, all the items I've listed in the coming pages. The real challenge in this changing of the gears is in the mindset of the parents and grandparents. Instead of looking at your child (or grandchild) as this neat little kid and enjoying every part of him or her, the focus should be on a time of preparation for what you want to see in the future.

The visible behavior you see is a reflection of the invisible, and oftentimes, the unresolved issues in the life of your teen.

Your focus must shift gears from a teaching model to a training model. Teaching is the gear all should be engaged in the first twelve years. Training is the next gear. Might I remind you that this is not automatic? It will not happen on its own or by itself. It's a determined conviction on the part of parents and grandparents, to push, allow, and focus on helping children take what they have been taught and put it into play in their life. Then, they can mature and develop out of the self-centered, entitled mindset, where they wake up in the morning and ask, "What's everyone going to do for me today?"

Move from Dependence on You to Developing Independence

Children are dependent on their parents for everything. If the goal is to help your teen develop healthy independence by the time they reach the age of eighteen, then the training has to happen now, as they leave childhood behind and enter adolescence. Teaching gives them the tools; training allows them to use them.

Chances are, everyone has been doing pretty much everything for your children up to this point. Someone has made all their decisions, taken responsibility for every area of their life, had total control of their behavior, given them all the answers, and lectured them until blue in the face. If you don't switch gears, you'll end up with that twenty-five-year-old I mentioned earlier.

Here are some examples that might help you understand this a little better. If children are taught about school, the need to do homework, and the importance of good grades, then at some point they must be allowed to determine when to study, hand in their own work, and even take the risk of failing. If and when they experience failure, they begin to learn that not everyone else is going to do the work for them. They must do it for themselves.

It's funny to have all the parents at the science fair laugh about how much work they put into their fourth graders' science projects. Parents come up with a good idea, do all the work, and pretty much oversee the whole project. It's really kind of funny. But it's not that funny when the kids hit the ninth grade. As a matter of fact, it would be rather sad. The problem is not the child. The parents are encouraging immaturity instead of taking the opportunity to encourage maturity.

Here is another example. From the ages of one to twelve years old, you have taught your children what to do in a particular situation. When you begin to switch to the training model, you move from telling them what they must do, to asking, "What do you think you ought to do?" Posing that question to them means they'll have to dig through their memory bank and pull out the file for what they were taught to do in that kind of situation. This is where parents and grandparents allow children to begin the critical thinking process. They hadn't had to think before because everyone did it for them. It is imperative this becomes their turn to figure it out, long before life forces them to do it on their own.

This training model means that instead of you (parent or grandparent) taking the ball and running with it, you toss it to them and let them run. Will they stumble? Sure they will, just like you did the first time you were given a chance to run with the ball. If they do stumble, they'll get back up, because you shifted gears from being a teacher and moved into the role of trainer. As the trainer on the sidelines, you encourage them to brush off their knees and keep going. Then, you cheer them on.

Move from *Your* Decisions
to Helping Them Learn to Make *Their* Decisions

Decision-making is important. If you want your teens to be able to make big and important decisions later on in life, you've got to give them the opportunity to flex their decision-making muscles. The more they work out now, the better shape they'll be in when they are truly out on their own. Is it easier, more time saving, and far more convenient to keep making the decisions ourselves? Absolutely. Does it stunt the growth of your teens' maturity? Absolutely.

Let them decide when they need to study for school. Now, if you have a child who can't stop playing video games or gets consumed with chatting or texting friends, then sure, you've got to intervene. Where there are no internal boundaries, parents have to establish external boundaries.

By thirteen years of age, it would greatly help a child to be able to decide what they are going to wear to school. At some point, they need to determine whether they're going to brush their teeth, wear sunscreen at the beach (kind of a learn or burn lesson), or purchase new clothes (even with your money).

It's hard to break them from being dependent upon you to make their own decisions, because it's easier for them to let you do it. Plus, if they make a mistake in their decisions, they might just blame the outcome on you, because you didn't do what you were supposed to do. You and I know that transferring the responsibility to make good decisions is a process. It will take time, but it is well worth the effort as your teen progresses through adolescence.

Where there are no internal boundaries, parents have to establish external boundaries.

Let your teens begin to decide where to eat dinner, what TV programs to watch, what time to go to bed, what music to listen to, and whether or not they play a sport. At some point, they will have to decide which church they go to or whether they go at all, who they're going to date, whether they need a job, how they spend their Saturdays, and who their friends will be.

Remember that the goal here is allowing them to flex those decision-making muscles while you're still around to ultimately help lift the weight off their chest if it falls. Then there is still time to have those deeper discussions about what happened when they made a mistake or a not-so-good choice and what they could do better next time. I'm not encouraging you, as a parent, to allow every decision to be made by your teen. There has got to be some home rules in place, so a child knows that some decisions have already been made for them. Yes, you do want your home to be a place of rest for your kids, but you don't want it to be a place that is out of control, where they get to do anything and everything they want. Rules without relationship may cause rebellion. Relationships without rules cause chaos.

Move from You Doing It to Them Doing It

Quit doing everything for them. Revolving our lives around our kids is easy. If entitlement and selfishness run rampant in a culture that is *all about me,* then you are the one to break that cycle. If you don't, then you will have spoiled brats on your hands who enter their twenties about to head into disaster. Their health may take a beating, lives may derail, or marriages may fail.

To help kids understand that I'm not their servant, maid, tutor, slave, or employee, I tell them, "I owe you nothing, but I want to give you everything. Still, I owe you nothing." It changes their perspective when I do things for them or help them in any way. I want them to be responsible for their own lives and break the habit of selfishness supported by their "me culture." Now, if I do anything for them or give them anything, it's an act of grace and not a fulfillment of obligation or entitlement. That is an important concept for them to embrace. It's an idea that will change their future relationships.

Rules without relationship may cause rebellion. Relationships without rules cause chaos.

In the teen years, it's time for them to start doing their own laundry. Let them pack for their own vacation. Let them choose their own hairstyle. Let them purchase their own clothes, no matter how awful they look. Let them put their own gas in the car. Let them learn how to use an alarm clock now, so you don't have eighteen-year-olds in college who can't get out of bed. Let them be responsible for their own academics, and let them take their own clothes to the cleaners.

Quit doing everything for them!

Move from Your Control to Their Control

The only way a child will learn to take control of his or her life and develop the need for self-control is by a parent or grandparent letting go.

Give teens control. In the early years, you have total control over your children. You make all their decisions, do everything for them, and have full responsibility for their lives. Changing gears can be hard at age thirteen when you begin to realize that you don't have as much control over them anymore. So give some of it over, before it gets wrestled away from you. It's much more effective and relationship-building that way.

Attempts to take control from them may prevent them from learning self-control. You want them to be in control, don't you? I do! I want my children to have self-control when they get pulled over by a policeman for speeding. I want them to have self-control with a girlfriend or boyfriend. I want them to learn restraint with their words when they're provoked. I want them to embrace the concept of keeping their mouths shut when it would be easier to fire off comments that will only cause more damage.

I tell the kids who live with us that I really don't care whether they pass or flunk their classes at our school. Isn't that a great thing to say to students, coming from a founder of a boarding school? If the truth were told, I do care. But I don't accept responsibility for their academics. I tell them they have control and can make the decision to complete high school whenever they want. It is my way of giving up control and giving it to them.

Move from Giving Answers to Asking Questions

As parents, we always have a comment, an answer, or the right way of doing things. Shoot, you know we do. It's because we're good, we know what's right, and if everyone would just do it our way, we'd all be better off. I chuckle as I write this because there is some truth in my comments. You and I can be the greatest deterrents to our teen's search for answers because we know all the answers. Ha!

I encourage you to do this: Quit being the answer man or answer woman. Begin to let your adolescents do some searching on their own. If they don't learn it now, they'll only have to learn it when they're apart from you. You're used to giving answers in their early years. That's what teaching is all about. Now that the gears are shifting in your parenting, you must stop giving the answers and start asking more questions to help your kids learn to process on their own. Your conversations should contain phrases like the following:

- What do you think we should do in this situation?
- What would you do if you were in that position?
- What do you think would be the best alternative to resolve this issue?
- Did you think that was fair?
- Would you have done the same thing?
- What do you think is the greatest struggle teens face today?
- What do you think about the legalization of marijuana?
- Do you think politics are as messy as they seem?

When your teen answers, hold your tongue and don't correct. Keep yourself from telling them where they are wrong. Refrain from sharing your opinion. Simply let the discussion happen. If they ask you what you think, even then, you should not always answer. Many times your answer will stop the conversation because you probably just shared the best answer. What else can your child add at that point? If you want them to come to the right answer themselves, let them figure it out. Don't give it to them.

Please beware of this: No manipulation! Don't ask questions so that you can listen to what they have to say and gain a platform to share your opinion. This is what I call *selfish questioning* because it's not really about your teen. It's more about your need to talk. Always ask questions. Quit giving the answers.

Move from Punishment
to Their Understanding of the Value in Discipline

Punishment used to be easy to dole out when your children were little—violate the home policy, get in trouble. It was all about following your rules and doing what you said without question. Punishment steered them away from wrong choices. It gave them understanding that good choices bring pleasure and foolish choices bring pain. Punishment kept foolish choices from happening or at least nipped them in the bud.

Now you're moving away from punishment into a world of discipline, with the end goal of self-discipline. Discipline now helps a child get to where they want to go and keeps them from ending up in a place they don't want to be. It's not about the infliction of pain. It emphasizes making good decisions.

Discipline lets adolescents and teens know you're working with them in their choices, to help, not to force them to do or not do things.

Discipline lets adolescents and teens know you're working with them in their choices, to help, not to force them to do or not do things. When teens know you're working with them and want to help get them to a better place in life, they'll welcome the limits, restrictions, and boundaries set around them. When they believe you're just out to punish them, they push back hard against your limits.

Move from Your Responsibility
to Encouraging Their Responsibility

Parents naturally make all decisions for infants and very young children. These young ones are totally dependent on adults for everything in life. As children grow, parents and grandparents still make the vast majority of decisions in their lives. If that pattern continues into the teen years, it fosters trouble for teens and the adults who love them. As kids enter their teen years, the greatest gift a parent or grandparent can give is to engage them in the process of making their own choices, so they can learn to accept responsibility for their own lives. This, in turn, will produce emotional, spiritual, and relational maturity.

Maturity is a by-product of responsibility. If anyone in the family prevents a child's acceptance of responsibility for his own life, then they are doing too much for that child (i.e., making too many decisions, keeping the control, and refusing to trust the child).

Luke 12:48 states something I believe is key to the training process:

From everyone who has been given much, much will be demanded; and from the one who has been entrusted with much, much more will be asked.

What I'm proposing in this training model is the transfer of quite a bit to your kids. While this means they'll experience more freedom in their pursuit of independence, it also means more will be required from your children.

Move from Lecturing to Having Discussions

This one is easy. Move from all those lectures that you realize are producing nothing and begin to have discussions that are full of opinions, questions, differing thoughts, and controversial stances. Remember, your discussions are no longer going to be little quips of words, where all the world's problems are solved in a few minutes. Most discussions are composed of many conversations, over a period of time. Often, you will not be able to solve any of the world's problems. And even if you think you can, it's wise to keep the solution to yourself and see if your teens can come to the same conclusion by themselves. Remember, you want to keep the conversation going. Your goal is to be a place of wisdom your child can visit over and over again.

Move from Telling to a Model of Sharing

Along the same vein of having discussions, movement from the teaching to the training model means a shift in the way you distribute what you have to say. It can no longer be, "This is the way it is. Period." It's got to be more like, "This is what I think," or "This is what I believe."

Many times when I ask teens if they want a response from me. I ask, "Do you want an answer or my opinion?" Sometimes they say, "Neither." I leave it at that. Successful parents with strong connections and relationships are okay leaving it right there. They know it creates a safe place for teens to hash out what they're trying to work out. It also leaves the door open for them to come back and ask for that advice or opinion later on if they can't figure it out.

Move from Talking to Listening

Here's another tough one. The times when you used to just talk to your kids needs to be replaced with spending more time listening once they enter their teen years. Many times, kids tell me that Mom and Dad just like to hear themselves talk and never listen to what they want to say. As one parent to another, you've had your time to talk. Now, it is your time to listen. Listen well to hear the heartbeat of your teens. You will never really understand them until you consider the world from their point of view. How would you rather be known? As one who talked all the time or one who was a great listener? Wise parents desire the latter.

Listen.

Move the Emphasis from *What You Do* to *Who You Are*

Making the transition from *what you do* for your kids, to *who you are* at your core, is an evolution and conversion for each parent. When you are "doing," it has more to do with behavior. When you shift to showing "who you are," you reveal your character. Many times, parents are more

34

concerned about the everyday, surface behavior they see and experience, rather than working on the heart and building their child's character. Parents can hone in on those occasional momentary glimpses of greatness and help their kids see it in themselves too.

A parent's voice of wisdom gives children the perspective that life is more than just a series of behaviors to be praised or corrected. Parents help their children understand that their greatness may feel locked inside for now, but it will soon be revealed in who they become. It's a message of hope and promise that can only come from a parent who is more concerned about where they are headed than where they have been.

> A parent's voice of wisdom gives children the perspective that life is more than just a series of behaviors to be praised or corrected.

As a final word about gear shifting from teaching to training, let me share this: Kids want to grow up. They want to take responsibility for their lives. They want to make decisions. They want to be mature. They want to be in control. They will always side with those who help them move toward independence and resist those who impede their progress. Make sure they side with you. Move over to the passenger side and hand over the keys of decision-making before you run out of gas. It may be a wild ride at first, but the journey is thrilling and the destination is well worth the price! It's a shifting of a style of parenting because your child is shifting to a new way of learning, as they move from concrete to abstract thinking. Their view of life is moving from the confines of the walls of your home to survival in a cruel world, which doesn't have their best interest in mind. So preparation becomes key, and a readiness to launch becomes a hidden desire—hidden in the heart of every child.

CHAPTER 3

Don't Save the Best for Last

For where your treasure is, there your heart will be also.

Luke 12:34 (KJV)

During the last ten years of my mom's life, she always told me how fast time flies and how it flies even faster with each passing day. Now that I'm in my sixties, I can comprehend what she was trying to tell me. It seems like I'm filling thirty-day prescriptions every other day. Sixty seconds seems like thirty. It feels like Christmas is every other month and my teeth are getting cleaned every other week. Life is sure speeding up.

Before you know it, that ol' body of yours will begin to wither, age will remind you of your limitations, and you'll be a number you never thought possible, wondering *where did all the time go?* The relentless marching on of the aging process will come at you through medical issues, gray hair, wrinkles, failing eyesight, droopy skin, and loss of hearing. Embracing the frailty of life and the promise of it one day ending can change who you are, how you are perceived, and the impact you will have on others. Everything you own will one day be given away. All your accumulations, money, collections, clothes, memorabilia—all of it—will be given away to family and friends, if not sold off to complete strangers. Comforting thought, isn't it?

After my mom died, we moved my dad into a retirement village because, as he put it, "The house is pretty quiet." We could all tell that the silence was taking a toll on him and would eventually drive him crazy. As we moved him into his new place, we moved out all the belongings he and my mom had acquired throughout their sixty-two years of marriage. I'm not sure why, but my dad stated all he needed to move to his new place was a couple of pieces of furniture, his clothes, his computer, and a pot to fix food in. Perhaps the loss of a spouse makes you realize how frivolous things are. He was reeling from his own grief and the prospect of now living life on his own in a new place with strangers around him. Who cared about doilies and knickknacks?

My siblings and I talked about what we each wanted from my parents' lifelong collection of belongings. Surprisingly, we didn't want much. Still, the thought of just giving it all away or selling it to others felt tough to process. I, too, grieved the loss of my mom and the change that was happening within our family now that she was gone. I rented a trailer and brought a ton of stuff home to Texas, where a few months later we had a garage sale and gave away much of my mom's history to people she never knew, families she never met, and strangers from countries she never visited. Then it hit me; the collection of all the stuff in our lives is just that—*stuff*.

I asked my kids what they wanted of mine when I died. My daughter couldn't think of anything. My son told me he wanted my guns and a few pairs of my boots. I remember saying, "That's it? That's all you want? Just those things?" He answered, "Yep, that's about it."

In 1974, I lost all my belongings to a tornado in Tulsa, OK. That event taught me about the value of things. My son's comments about what he wanted from my belongings showed me what holds true value. It isn't all the *stuff* I've been collecting all my life, any more than what my mom gathered during hers. The most valuable things in life aren't things at all. They're the relationships people form during their time on Earth. The pursuit of things (stuff) is frivolous; the pursuit of relationships is fundamental to God's plan for us all. I believe God desires us to invest our time, our resources, and our efforts in relationships.

So here's my first piece of advice in this chapter: Give it away. Give your time, your resources, and your efforts to those around you. In particular, give to your teens while they have the time to appreciate it and you have your health to enjoy the giving. Now, I'm one who believes in taking care of yourself financially. I'm a finance guy from the University of Tulsa who embraces what John

> God desires us to invest our time, our resources, and our efforts in relationships.

Wesley stated a couple of centuries ago, that one should, "Earn all you can, save all you can, give all you can." I'm a believer in financial security, especially as one enters retirement. But I'm all about sharing as well, and there is nothing more rewarding or more impactful than sharing with your family. Here's a proverb for all you parents and grandparents.

A good person leaves an inheritance for their children's children. (Proverbs 13:22)

I'm convinced of this. And I'm also convinced this verse isn't just talking about leaving money, if it's talking about that at all. It's about leaving a legacy, an heirloom, a tradition, and a heritage—something that lasts in the souls of your kids.

If you've picked up by now that I think your kids' teen years are the time when you can have the greatest influence when they need it the most, you are hearing me correctly. You can leave a valuable inheritance, while you are still alive, in the form of memorable events that are magnificent and meaningful. I encourage you to look for opportunities to experience life together with your kids, especially during the teen years. Find experiences that will give you memories to share, photos to post, opportunities to have life-on-life involvement, times of laughter together, and chances to build deeper relationships through common activities.

It's been said that the moods of a lifetime are found in the all-but-forgotten experiences of adolescence. I know this to be true after listening to thousands of teens share the unforgettable experiences that shaped their lives and determined their destinies.

Personally, as I reflect on my childhood, I'm not sure I remember too many of those experiences. Many times I wondered what it would have been like to have a heart full of memories of experiences with my parents and grandparents. I've speculated at what I could have done earlier in my life if

It's been said that the moods of a lifetime are found in the all-but-forgotten experiences of adolescence.

someone had given me a thousand dollars when I got married and how that would have helped in so many ways. I've pondered what it would have been like to have my grandparents give me something that was dear to them; something passed on that meant something to them. I've wondered what messages I would have gotten if a parent had given me advice, taken the time to help in some fashion, or shown me an example of what it was like to value relationships and how to give.

My grandkids and the teens that live with us challenge me to think about whether I am doing those very things today. The times I wondered what I would have received have now been transformed into thinking about whether I am giving and changing the teens in my world with my time, resources, and efforts. That's how a parent or grandparent influences the life of their teen.

Here's my second piece of advice for this chapter: Don't wait. Don't save the best for last. You might just miss it. This story gives clarity to what I mean.

David Muth and I met when his daughter came to live with us at

Heartlight ten years ago. We hit it off the moment we met. His winsome personality was a joy to be around, and his love for his family was attractive. His common sense was welcomed wisdom wrapped in his warm sense of humor. We laughed. We laughed a lot together. David knew I love wine, and we shared bottles of specialty wines throughout the years whenever we got together. We sent wine to each other on holidays or birthdays. Sitting on my back porch, we figured out the deep, hidden issues of life, God, and the souls of men, over glasses of fine wine. We had the kind of deep discussions I don't have with many. David collected wine and always told me about the bottles he was saving for a special occasion. I'm sure I added a few to his *special occasion* collection, all neatly and precisely tucked away for exclusive times of honor and celebration.

David and his wife, Amy, served on our board of directors at Heartlight, which sometimes felt like an excuse to get together and catch up on our very different lives. His life was the busy hospital life of an anesthesiologist. Mine was the founder of a ranch for struggling teens. David called me one afternoon to share that he had just been diagnosed with Parkinson's disease. As he described it, this was the Parkinson's that wasn't the *shaky* kind, but one that, over time, would deteriorate the organs in his body. He shared that most people with his diagnosis didn't live more than five or six years. He was going to have to retire at fifty-two and planned to move to Anna Maria Island, Florida, where he would face the challenges of his remaining years with Parkinson's.

After a couple of years of keeping up over the phone, getting updates on his condition, I decided I needed to spend some time with him at his home in Florida. I committed to doing so every couple of months. I'd travel to see him at the tail end of speaking engagements or make a stopover in Tampa on the way back home. The first time I got there to see him and Amy, I took him a beautiful three-hundred-dollar bottle of wine (Opus). He tucked it away in his wine stash, saving it for a special occasion. At that point in his Parkinson's journey, we always pulled out bottles not designated for special occasions and enjoyed them over the same deep discussions. We also watched movies and laughed until our bellies hurt.

Over time, Parkinson's took more and more of a toll on my dear friend. On one of my trips to see him, he said, "Let's take out one of those bottles I've been saving for a special occasion and have that tonight." He let me know that he had a 1960 Port, a bottle that was fifty-five years old and was his Cadillac of wines. He spent most of his adult life waiting to drink it. I felt privileged to be the recipient of this special occasion.

Don't save for that *special occasion* because the *special occasion* is today.

His hands had gotten to where he couldn't open the bottle, and he asked me to do the honors. As I opened the bottle and began to pour the wine, we were both quick to notice the wine had gone bad. Basically, it had turned to mush. The look of disappointment on his face is one I will never forget. All the hope he held onto for so many years of enjoying that special bottle of wine was dashed. Next, he said, "Well, I have a 1968 Bordeaux (French) I've been saving." I opened it up and much to our surprise, it had gone bad as well. He continued, "Well, I have a 1974 Barolo I've been saving for a special occasion. Let's open up that one." We did, and much to our shock, it had gone bad as well. "Well, I have a 1992 Screaming Eagle from Napa I've been saving for a special occasion. Let's give that one a shot." We did, and to our dismay, the same scenario repeated itself. David began to realize that what he had been saving for was all in vain. After a couple more bottles of wine brought the same ending, I asked David if we could just open the bottle I brought him months ago—that Opus I gave him for a special occasion. He relented, and we both enjoyed.

That night, as I lay awake in David and Amy's guest bedroom, I kept thinking over and over what lesson was to be learned from what had just happened. This is what I concluded: Don't save for that *special occasion* because the *special occasion* is today. The fact that we were both together that day was occasion enough to enjoy the very best. I committed to this. Anytime someone comes to my home, and we share wine, I'm going to pull out the very best and most expensive bottle of wine I have and serve it. I'm not going to wait for any *special occasion* because that *special occasion* is now. This moment.

Catch what I'm saying? Don't wait. Your teens need you now.

Time passes way too quickly not to take advantage of the present that is today.

Don't wait until you're no longer busy; that will never happen.

Don't wait until that special occasion; it is happening around you every day.

Don't wait until you can afford it; you can't afford *not* to.

Don't wait until you can find the time; it passes way too quickly.

Don't miss opportunities during your teen's years; it will be gone too soon.

You will never be appreciated more or have a greater impact at any other time than the *special occasion* that is before you today.

CHAPTER 4

How to Give Big-Picture Perspective to Your Teen's World

The beginning of wisdom is this: Get wisdom. Though it cost all you have, get understanding.

Proverbs 4:7

Taylor Swift is one of the best-selling country/pop artists of all time. She is the recipient of ten Grammy Awards, twenty-one Billboard Music Awards, eleven Country Music Association Awards, and countless other awards too many to list. All the accolades meant nothing to my two granddaughters. They were just dying to see this popular artist perform. When they found out T-Swizzle was coming to a venue just a few miles from where we all lived, no one would rest until tickets were secured.

My daughter was charged with purchasing the tickets, which she quickly did just before the concert sold out. The day came, and the five of us set off for the concert; two little girls dressed like Taylor, one mom wanting to please her kids, and two grandparents who love country music and wanted to see this phenomenon named Taylor.

Jan and I have been to quite a few concerts throughout our lives, and the challenge of each ticket purchase is to get as close to the front of the venue as possible or at least reasonably close enough to recognize the performer as something more than just a dot on the stage. Ever since our first date to a Led Zeppelin concert in 1971, Jan has always asked, "Did you get good seats?" Of course I would glow with pride in sharing how close we would be to the artists and how great our seats would be. I love the front-row view at any concert.

My daughter didn't have this in mind when she purchased the tickets for the Taylor Swift concert. When we entered the 14,000-seat arena, we trudged up and up to our seats, further and further from the stage, finally ending up in the top section in the very last row of seats. I mean, the back of my head was touching concrete. You couldn't get any further back. There I sat, the only man in the whole arena, in the worst seats in the house. The stage appeared to be over a mile away.

I looked at my daughter with *What-are-these-seats?* kind of look, and she told me these were the only tickets she was able to purchase. Then came the now famous and unforgettable statement. Macie, my five-year-old granddaughter, looked around and said with wonder, "Poppa, these are the best seats in the whole place. You can see everything from here!"

Perspective. It was all in the perspective—that big-picture view that helps you see more than what is evident and beyond that which is right before you.

For teens today, perspective has been lost. The impact of today's actions on one's later life, the results of poor choices, and the consequences for not following rules are largely ignored because parents have lost their ability to influence their kids through giving them a *bigger picture* perspective in their parenting relationship.

Moms and Dads have moved from parenting to *peer-enting* in an attempt to create a relational environment that was perhaps not present when they were raised. That movement, coupled with a teen's perception of not needing to respect and support those in authority, has now *cut the legs off* of mom's and dad's ability to guide and influence. Teens now rely more on their peers than they do their parents, creating a blind-leading-the-blind scenario that hardly fosters maturity, barely encourages responsibility, and certainly can't be a great fountain of wisdom.

Psychologist and family physician Leonard Sax states in his wonderful and insightful book, *The Collapse of Parenting*,

> The most serious consequence of the shift from a parenting-oriented culture to a peer-oriented culture is that parents no longer are able to provide that big picture to their children. (Sax, 198)

See where I'm headed?

I'm not saying parents are ineffective in their parenting. I spend two hundred nights a year on the road leading parenting conferences around the country in an attempt to help moms and dads better understand the teen world and how to counter this contrary culture working overtime to undermine their parenting roles. I do believe that parents have to be relational in their approach to their teens. They can't lead in such an authoritarian way that it pushes their child away. Instead, they need to use their God-given authority in a relational way to lead and empower their teens to be respecters of the whole family structure, and they need backup.

You must develop an understanding of what is happening in your teen's culture, and help them see beyond what is right in front of them.

We've already stated that we're glad we don't have to grow up in this adolescent culture. I know I would have been a mess in my junior high school years if I had access to some of the imagery and information that our kids are exposed to on a daily basis.

Well, your kids have to grow up in this culture. They have to function and survive in a world that is different from the world their parents and grandparents grew up in. That doesn't mean it is worse or bad or doomed. It just means it's different. Different means you must approach your kids from a different angle, one that allows you to be invited to speak truth into their lives. Not only must you develop an understanding of what is happening in their culture, but you also have to possess the ability to see beyond what is right in front of them and offer a voice of wisdom to guide and direct your kids. You can help them understand the purpose and the reasons behind what you are asking of them. You can give them *big-picture* perspective. They may have the Internet, but you have experience. They may be able to ask Siri or Alexa, but no newfangled gadget can speak the truth about the meaning of life, love, and relationships. You can.

The world they live in is quite different from the one we grew up in, but it's all they know. What is totally foreign to you is absolutely common to them. Gaining an understanding of their world and culture (without condemning or criticizing it) helps in your approach to drawing them to you as a source of wisdom.

> Gaining an understanding of their world and culture helps in your approach to drawing them to you as a source of wisdom.

Let me share a few of the challenges our teens face today. Not only is there a lack of respect for authority, but there is also an extreme lack of respect for one another. Media depicts politicians, pastors, police officers, teachers, administrators, businessmen and women, coaches, priests, and parents as people not worthy of respect. The current American (really, Western) culture encourages voicing disrespect of anything and anyone you don't agree with. Political correctness hampers the ability to speak freely, and the *rights of all* have so far encouraged more division than unity.

The difficulty with this culture of disrespect is that the wisdom that can be obtained from people in authority has already been tossed out before any can be transferred.

The amount of information at everyone's fingertips has overloaded our lives. Think about the number of sources of information you had when you were growing up—three main TV stations, a newspaper, and the radio. Now there are countless ways to find out everything about anything you want. The need to get information from friends and family is almost nil. Teens today are stuffed with information, yet starving for wisdom.

Think about it. Communication is at our fingertips twenty-four hours a day, seven days a week. Text messaging, apps, social media, and image messaging sites are changing the way people communicate. Dating sites now account for over fifty percent of the marriages in the U.S. Millions of pictures are sent on a daily basis, millions of videos posted on anything you can think of. Social networking sites are changing the social structure of the adolescent world, providing a false sense of connection with one another. Pornography and sexually explicit videos are readily available, changing the rules of modesty and permissible sexual behavior.

Teens live in a culture where alternative lifestyles are promoted, prominent, and prevalent. Gender confusion abounds. Young men hardly know what it means to be a man, and young girls struggle to know what it is to be a woman.

There is an extreme absence of role models. Teens are becoming frailer. Everyone wants to be famous. Adolescents are moving more and more towards being overweight, out of shape, and suicidal. More kids are on medication than ever before.

As a parent, you can spend time with your teens arguing any one of the above points, sharing everything that is wrong with this teen culture, but that won't build the relationship. Even though it's all true, you will accomplish nothing, except to send a clear message that you are disconnected, a *fuddy-duddy* (Does that term even still exist?), an old-timer lost in a new generation, or one who is just clueless. Yes, you can spend all your time criticizing their culture, but it will get you nowhere.

Do you have pet peeves? I have pet peeves. There are some things that just bug me and seem odd to me. I know it's a part of getting older, but there are just some elements of this culture that scream, "Danger, Will Robinson, danger!" to me. I know it's a result of this performance-driven and appearance-focused world we live in.

Here's what bugs me: It feels like people are trying to outdo and outshine each other on the Internet, seeking the false approval of social media followers instead of building real relationships with loved ones right in front of them. There are individual posts on Internet social networking sites that scream, "Will someone just look at me? Will someone just value me?"

I see a dad and daughter in a video from her wedding doing a special dance that sometimes seems like it has little to do with celebration and more to do with the need for attention. I see kids going to proms that have very little to do with wanting to dress up and more about showing off. I see pictures and videos of couples' wedding showers that just seem odd to me. It seems like every pregnancy now automatically comes with a *gender reveal* party. And don't get me started on the videos of people getting engaged that sometimes seem more about putting on an over-the-top show than about recording a special moment of their love for each another.

Am I revealing my age a bit? I'm sure you can list some things that bug you as well. Your pet peeves may differ from my list, but I think we all have things that bother us. Here's the best way I can handle those cultural differences and things I don't always agree with—I can keep my mouth shut. Why on earth would I do that? Why would I let my grandkids and this culture get away with all this *nonsense* when I know better? Because the Bible tells me so.

Even fools are thought wise when they keep silent; with their mouths shut, they seem intelligent. (Proverbs 17:28, NLT)

Yep, sometimes we communicate loudest and smartest when we say nothing at all. Your role as a parent isn't to point out everything that's wrong with this country, this culture, or the way the world is going. Your role is to give a different perspective to your kids' world, that to us, appears to have gone crazy, but to them is normal.

Again, it starts with first understanding the world they live in and the value of your role in their lives. You can't be a clueless outsider who just drops in from time to time with what you think is wisdom but sounds to them like a whole lot of uninformed criticism. If you don't understand, it will hamper your relationship, which prevents the transfer of

Sometimes we communicate loudest and smartest when we say nothing at all.

biblical truths, principles, wisdom, and stories that carry on the legacy of your family.

Teens live in a world searching for someone, anyone, to listen and watch. They long for someone who understands the world and will help them understand it. They need someone who looks at life from a bigger-picture perspective and compassionately communicates the path to take to avoid mistakes and choices that could negatively affect their lives.

Perspective.

Oh yeah, back to that Taylor Swift concert. We were sitting in the back, right? My head was banging against the concrete as 13,997 little girls around me screamed at the top of their lungs throughout the whole show. Remember, these were the worst seats in the house (from my perspective). My little Macie, bless her heart, thought they were the best.

Forty-five minutes into the concert, my perspective changed too. Much to our surprise, Taylor Swift suddenly stood singing ten feet away from us. She had come to the back (the very back) of the venue to sing right to everyone seated a million miles away from the stage. (I now see why so many adore this young lady; she loves her fans.)

Macie looked at me, eyes shining, and said, "See, Poppa, I told you these were the best seats!" She was right.

They were the best seats in the house.

It was all in the perspective.

CHAPTER 5

A Parent's Greatest Challenge

Spend time with the wise and you will become wise, but the friends of fools will suffer.

Proverbs 13:20 (NCV)

People have a propensity to complain about the youth of *today*. They always have. Throughout history, one can easily find moanings and groanings about these *young people* and how their attitudes and actions are destroying the very moral fiber of our country. We, meaning any of us who are older than teenagers and millennials, tend to recall our time of adolescence as a wonderful time of innocence and wonder. Nothing we did was *that bad,* certainly not as damaging and destructive as the practices of youth today. We adopt an all-is-lost attitude, thinking we are living in the worst times there have ever been.

When I think back to the time I grew up in New Orleans in the 1960s, I vividly remember the Beatles (I saw them in City Park on September 16, 1964.), the Beach Boys, the first man to walk on the moon, *The Ed Sullivan Show*, *Mary Poppins*, *The Beverly Hillbillies*, Walt Disney, Debbie Meyer swimming in the 1968 Olympics in Mexico City, Woodstock, James Bond movies, and *The Dirty Dozen*, just to name a few memories. That's what instantly comes to my mind.

When I reflect more deeply, I remember what else went on during the '60s. I come to the somewhat different conclusion that perhaps those good ol' days weren't as good as I thought. Vietnam, the assassination of President John F. Kennedy, the later assassination of his brother Sen. Bobby Kennedy, the assassination of Martin Luther King Jr., Louisiana's Hurricane Camille, the Bay of Pigs, the Manson murders, riots in Chicago and Detroit. Not the good ol' days, but days and years when an entire nation experienced a huge cultural shift.

Maybe it wasn't so good back then. Maybe, just maybe, it's not so bad now. Times are different. Very different. But different doesn't warrant instant judgment. Positive change rarely comes out of negative criticism. In other words, complaining doesn't fix anything. Complaining about the youth of today is nothing new. This is what Peter the Hermit said in a sermon he preached during his lifetime.

> The world is passing through troublous times. The young people of today think of nothing but themselves. They have no reverence for parents or old age. They are impatient of all restraint. They talk as if they knew everything, and what passes for wisdom with us is foolishness with them. As for the girls, they are forward, immodest and unladylike in speech, behavior, and dress.

French priest Peter the Hermit played a key role during the First Crusade and delivered this sermon (and his perspective on youth) more than five hundred years ago!

If you're like me, you don't want to complain all the time about the culture of teens today. Who wants to be seen as crotchety or decrepit instead of fun and cool? I want to understand today's youth culture, not frame it as an evil culture with no hope. If I see it like that, not only am I judging those kids that live with us (at Heartlight), my grandkids, and their friends, but also what hope will they have for their own futures?

I want to understand, so I can help my kids navigate through today's times, which seem so different from the world I grew up in. Yet, they are so similar in their challenges. One of the major challenges remains to bring timeless truth and wisdom to an ever-changing world of influence. This challenge is not the sole goal of parenting. First and foremost, the intent is to connect with your children during their teen years. You can be the connection who offers hope.

Deep engagement isn't inherited; it's cultivated. You cultivate it every time you are intentional in reaching out to your teen.

You can complain about today's youth. However, complaining always blocks the connection. Instead, I suggest you pursue ways of connecting that will move your children to bond with you so strongly that you will be able to offer them what they cannot get from any other person in the world.

I've found connection doesn't automatically happen because you are a parent. Deep engagement isn't inherited; it's cultivated. You cultivate it every time you are intentional in reaching out to your children in ways that make them want to reach back. When you are intentional about asking for an invitation into their world instead of trying to drag them out of it and into yours, you can help your children get to the places they want to be. You can also help keep them from ending up in places they don't want to be.

This process begins with parents asking questions. Hopefully, it then blossoms into a relationship where the child asks the questions. This exchange is a process, one I've learned from my relationships with thousands of teens.

There are five necessary steps in this process of engagement and connection with your adolescent (and sometimes older) kids. Let's unpack them a little here.

Show Interest

During the first years of our kids' lives, I think we get involved for our own selfish reasons. We love their cuteness, enjoy watching them grow, feel ecstatic when they give us a name (no matter how corny or funny those names may be). Babies make us feel good, look good, and put a smile on our face. I don't think there's anything wrong with our intentions at this point. Pride in your progeny (once removed) is pretty normal.

Then those cute little kids turn twelve, and it all begins to change. That is exactly when parents better change right with them. Adolescence is a critical point that could determine your level of involvement in the rest of their lives. During this critical time, you have to shift the focus of your relationship from your interests to theirs.

If your child feels for a moment that your purpose and intent in their life is just to transfer all the wisdom you've gained in life, you will bore them to tears. You will quickly find yourself irrelevant in their lives. It will be apparent to them that you are in this thing to fulfill your own agenda, not because you care about them. They will see it as nothing more than another program that is more about you than them. They can smell that a mile away. You may think adolescents and teens have no common sense, but they can be incredibly savvy. And they can quickly spot a fake. Remember, parenting is not about you. It's about your kids.

Adolescence is a critical point that could determine your level of involvement in the rest of their lives.

Paul writes about this when he says to the Philippians,

> *Do nothing out of selfish ambition or vain conceit. Rather, in humility value others above yourselves, not looking to your own interests but each of you to the interests of the others.* (Philippians 2:3-4)

The second part of this *shifting* is changing the focus of your interest. One of the hardest challenges of parenting is sharing the wisdom you have gathered through life in a way that applies to *their* world and *their* culture, not the world you grew up in and learned from.

I know teens show an interest in me because I have an interest in them. They are longing for someone to listen to their hearts and their stories. They want to be loved and cared for beyond the five love languages. They want to do things together. They want to eat where they want to eat, go where they want to go, and have someone help them fulfill

Showing interest in your kids isn't something you do; it must become who you are.

their dreams. Showing interest in your kids isn't something you do; it must become who you are.

Adapt to Their World

Okay, so you live in a world of immodest girls who are unladylike in their behavior, foolish boys who think only of themselves, and a world where kids have a great sense of entitlement. They are impatient, know everything, and hardly respect their elders. That is exactly how Peter the Hermit saw it way back around A.D. 1080. That is the world of kids today, and in every age, it seems. But it's the world your kids have to live in.

Those are the cards you've been dealt. They're more than just cards; they're the kids you love. If you want to be an influence and make an impact on their lives, then you will have to adapt your message so it includes an understanding of the world they live in.

When I say adapt, I'm not telling you to scrap your standards or beliefs and discard what you hold to be true and valuable. I am telling you that your message has to apply to their world. You, or your message, can't be a stick in the mud, but pliable and adjustable to wrap around the issues they are facing. Usually, people who criticize the cards they've been dealt, can't adapt. That gives them very little ability to speak into the lives of their teen children.

You'll be like the major department stores and companies we see going belly up. They couldn't adapt to the changing times and keep up with the transformation and conversion of a culture that has made some pretty extreme shifts in the last few years. So they closed up shop. Don't close the doors on the teens you love.

If your message is relevant, don't change your content. But do change the way you approach it and say it, so the intended recipients of the message can embrace the message, engage with applicability, and value the effectiveness of the wisdom shared.

As I travel across North America, I see a great decline in church attendance by those about to graduate from high school and those in their late teens. In other words, there are about a million kids in the seventh-grade youth program and about four who remain in the church by their senior year. Okay, I may be exaggerating and joking a little here, but there is a major drop. This age group tends to take a hiatus from church, and I think they do so for a couple of adaptability reasons.

The first reason is that many teens believe the church isn't that important. The busyness of their schedules, coupled with other interests, crowds out time for church and church-related activities. The second reason is that youth leaders have been slow to adapt the gospel message to an age group that has gone through major, radical upheavals in its socialization process. I'm not faulting youth guys (or gals). The immense and rapid changes within the youth culture caught them off guard. But these two reasons speak volumes to the need for the adaptability of the message to a new, tech-savvy but relationship-poor generation, often overwhelmed by life as they know it.

Adaptability is more than the pastor wearing an untucked shirt and ripped or even skinny jeans. It's more than current and contemporary worship songs with lights down low and a few candles burning through the fog machine. It is understanding the needs and speaking directly to the issues that teens are facing, then giving directives that speak directly to those problems and matters in a way that doesn't alienate teens.

Here's the challenge for most parents. Whether we like it or not, we're the pioneer parents of this generation. We, as parents, are trying to figure out how this "tech world" of smart phones and excessive access to information, plays out in our family structure. It's a new world for our kids that is becoming their new normal. And it's a new world for parents trying to fit their "normal" into what many of us would consider "abnormal." It's a challenge, but one that we must pioneer and figure out if we are to adapt the message of our hearts to the life of our teens.

Build Relationship

A real relationship takes the investment of time, effort, and resources as mentioned earlier in this book. The key word is *investment*. The focus of that investment has to be the benefit of your teen, motivated out of love for that child.

Paul wrote to the Thessalonians and said,

We loved you so much that we shared with you not only God's Good News but our own lives, too. (1 Thessalonians 2:8)

Teens are looking for genuineness, authenticity, and relationships that offer something more than only correction when they mess up. They desire someone who is frank, honest, and isn't afraid to speak the truth in love because they know the motivation comes from a deep empathy for their plight.

If you have a discipline problem, you have a relationship problem. If you have a respect problem, you have a relationship problem. If you have an obedience problem, you have a relationship problem. In a relationship, you will see the problems, and in a relationship, you will discover a teen's motivation for change. A teen does not change because of an authoritarian approach. A teen listens to authority because of relationship.

Your relationship with your children could be the only voice of wisdom they listen to, in a time of their lives when they aren't listening to God.

The need to have fun together is paramount. How much you laugh together is a good measure of your relationship. The amount of communication between you and your children will be an indicator of how healthy your relationship is.

So learn every way possible to communicate hope and perspective. Be sure to try to keep up with technology so you maintain and entertain new forms of communication. If you don't know how to do this, ask the kids. They'll be happy to teach you, and it will give you an opportunity to learn something new together.

Create Connection

The connection I'm talking about is the next step in the relationship with your child. This connection is more than you making things happen. It's when communication, effort, and desire to spend time together become a two-way street. This is what you want to happen with your teenage children. It is more important than the message you have to share. It has to be cultivated…and watered…and fertilized…and allowed to grow.

Your relationship with your children could be the only voice of wisdom they listen to, in a time of their lives when they aren't listening to God.

Let me give you an example. My granddaughter Maile and I love country music. She knows the lyrics to every current country song. How she does it, I'll never know. Because of her love for this genre of music, I joined the Country Music Association so we could attend the Country Music Awards every year. I purchase the tickets, book the flight, and we go. We laugh, take pictures, laugh more, cheer on the artists, and leave Nashville with memories that will last her a lifetime. I purchase shirts and programs for her and provide opportunities for her to meet as many artists as I can. It's all for one purpose—to keep the connection we've found and hopefully nurture it until my dying day.

We text each other with news about upcoming concerts and up-and-coming artists. We look together for the next opportunity to spend time at these events. The result? A special connection that ties our hearts together. It is a tie that binds when other things in her life aren't quite as she hopes they'd be. The connection has been a lifeline for Maile and me.

So here are some things I've learned about connection with kids:

- Connection is more than just a relationship (Anyone can have that!); it's a conduit for providing hope and direction.
- Connection is not just making sure you have a great Christmas picture of all your family to send out to friends.
- Connection is not measured by the number of pictures you post of your child on your social networking sites.
- Connection is not just appearing to have a relationship; connection is having the relationship that is measured by two-way efforts to remain engaged with one another.
- Connection is not an opportunity for correction.
- Connection is a mutual love for one another established because a parent determines to pour life and love into a child who longs to be connected.

Invite Questions

When I initially show interest in any teen, including my grandkids, I do it by asking questions about his or her life, thoughts, and heart. It's not the interrogating type of questioning that puts them on the spot or makes them feel like I'm looking for problems, but the type of questions that convey value.

The questions I ask also give them an example of what it is like to show interest in others, to consider others more important than oneself.

My hope is they'll begin to ask me questions because they see me as a parent full of wisdom (not correction), one who is genuinely focused on bettering their lives, and one who is willing to put his money where his mouth is and share time, effort, and resources to further the relationship.

This is what I want to happen: I want them to start asking me questions. You'll know you have a connection when your kids start asking in some shape or form any of the following questions:

- Can I tell you something?
- Hey, want to get together for dinner?
- Hey Dad, did you ever smoke pot or get drunk?
- Hey Mom, did you and Dad ever have sex before you got married?
- Dad, what if I marry the wrong person?
- Mom, did you ever fall away from Jesus...I mean, just not get it sometimes?
- Hey, what's the one life lesson you've found to be the most important?

As a parent, this is what you've been waiting for. It's their invitation to you to speak the truth (however painful that may be) into their lives. They're asking because they want answers. Their questions will let you know there is a connection, and they want wisdom.

Over time, you'll find that talking about the hard stuff and sharing the reality of the lessons you've learned will convey those rare qualities of good relationships called genuineness and authenticity—two items in high demand in today's teen culture.

They are learning. You can be a safe place, a sounding board as they learn how to function in their culture in a healthy way. They're just doing it differently than you did. I assure you they will learn what they need to learn to survive in their world. Hopefully, they'll do it with a foundation of wisdom that you speak into their lives, so their learning isn't quite as painful as your acquisition of wisdom was. It's one of the greatest challenges of parents, but so well worth the effort.

Quit complaining about your kids. Begin the trek to building a relationship that connects you to the very heart of your children. Remember, it's not about what you *do*, and it's not necessarily about what you *say*. It's more about who you *are* in the presence of your kids that has the greatest influence.

CHAPTER 6

Why Gray Hair Works to Your Benefit

The glory of young men is their strength, but the splendor of old men is their gray hair.

Proverbs 20:29 (ESV)

As I see grandparents take up the role of parenting their grandkids, I can't help but feel the need to include a chapter that speaks to the role that grandparents play in the life of their teen grandkids. Personally, I believe that grandkids are a reward for not killing your own kids, and the importance of a grandparent's involvement in the life of their family is paramount. So, this chapter is for you, and might help show you the role you can play in helping your teen grandkids get through this contrary culture.

What do your grandkids call you?

Soon-to-be grandparents wrangle over what they want to be called. I tell them it doesn't matter what the kids call you. You'll love whatever name they attach to you.

I've heard some crazy ones, just to prove my point. Who would have thought that some grandparents would be called any of these following names and like it?

Busoma, BooBoo, Oompa, Suggy, Bop-Bop, Botchie, Amma, GaGa,

Bearbsie and Poppa Bear, Bla-Bla (now, that's an interesting one), Birdie, Big Grandpa, Bomp, and of course, Bobaloo.

Call grandparents whatever you want, make fun of all the various nicknames, but when that child calls you by that special name, there's just something that makes a grandparent feel wanted and needed.

My grandkids call me *Poppa* in front of me. I'm sure they say other things behind my back. But *Poppa* pretty much gets my full attention. Once I was in Moscow, Russia, a young girl ran up to me and said, "Poppa!" Evidently, that's a common word for fathers in Russia, and she immediately had my attention. She then said, "Take me!" She said only three words, but because she said "Poppa," she had my immediate attention. I felt I should do whatever she said. I even called Jan and told her we should adopt her. There's something special that happens when you hear the name you were given by a grandchild.

Whatever your grandchildren call you, I'm sure it's a term of endearment that means a lot to you. I mean, who else could call you Birdie and Bop-Bop, introduce you to their friends like that, and get away with it? Ha! Why even my oldest granddaughter's friends call me *Poppa*. There's something about that position in their lives I don't want to lose.

Maybe it's the gray hair that attracts kids to me. Or maybe it's the mustache I wear from the 1880s that reassures them they're talking to an old guy who might just have some answers or give some understanding to anything confusing. I want to think I've earned every one of my gray hairs. I'm proud of them even though when they began showing up on my head I plucked them out as if embarrassed to be getting older. Proverbs 16:31 (NRSV) affirms my love of my gray hair: "Gray hair is a crown of glory; it is gained in a righteous life." Darn right, it is. And I'm going to use it any way I can to benefit those around me.

When I was a Young Life leader, I thought I would lose my effectiveness by age twenty-five. I thought maybe I would be too old at that age. Then as a youth minister, I thought my gig would be up at thirty when I crossed over the hill. When kids came to live with Jan and me at Heartlight, I began to think, "Okay, by forty, kids will stop listening to me." In my forties, I thought the half-century mark would close down the stream of teens coming to me to talk. Then I turned fifty, and one day as I was plucking out gray hairs, it occurred to me, I was no longer a *young thang* that kids wanted to talk to. I was a guy who was showing his age and teens actually wanted more.

Now that I'm in my sixties, I've come to realize that age and a little gray hair (actually, a lot of it) is a magnet for teens who want wisdom. Now I'm working hard to keep all this gray stuff I have. I've put away the tweezers and feel pretty comfortable with this aging process. It affords me a different spot in the lives of my grandkids, which they can get from no one else.

They're searching for wisdom. What they are getting from their peers, television, and the Internet is an overwhelming flow of information that doesn't always have substance. It's easy to find information, but not context or truth. Siri, Alexa, or anyone who has a smart phone can tell you what time it is or help you

Give them what they can't find anywhere else by maintaining a special connection with them that is irreplaceable and offers wisdom.

order a pizza. They can't help you ponder the real meaning of life or how a lifelong relationship really works. I want to give them what they can't find anywhere else by maintaining a special connection with them that is irreplaceable and offers wisdom—wisdom that takes into account the faults, struggles, makeup, genetics, history, tradition, and difficulties within this thing called *family*. Wisdom shared with perspective.

Wisdom is so much more than a collection of astute and sensible words shared at the right time. Teens have heard enough words through the bombardment of information. They desire for the "word to become flesh" (see John 1:14) and to see the application of all they have been taught through the years. It's basically their plea of, "Don't tell me. Show me."

Granddad, or whatever name you go by, don't worry that you're not saying the right thing. Many men feel inadequate like they lack wise words to share at the right time. That's okay. Your teen grandkids aren't buying the words they hear any more; they want to see those words in action.

Grandmas, or if your grandkids call you Amma or Bop-Bop (great names, eh?), it's not about your words once they reach the teen years. Quit talking so much and start showing them how your words line up with your actions. Talk less. Show more.

Here are the ways teens pick up wisdom:

1. Observation

They're watching you. In their quietness and cognitive processing, your grandkids are seeing whether your actions support the words you say. It's how they determine if the truth they hear is truthful enough to be fleshed out in real life.

They watch you in your everyday interactions with others, like drivers, waitresses, flight attendants, fellow workers, employees, landscapers, and those you do business with. They witness how you talk to your spouse, how you treat the dog, how you handle conflict, how much you laugh, how much you cry, and how much you hurt. They look at what you look at, what you read, how you care for folks who have less than you, how you treat other kids, and how you act toward those who hurt you and those who love you.

They are processing traits like forgiveness, grace, love, empathy, sympathy, encouragement, boldness, and integrity by comparing what they see against what they've been taught for so many years.

In order to see and observe, it's imperative that time is spent together. One can't see what isn't there. Presence (not presents) is key to having an impact on the life of your grandkids and maintaining that relationship through their teen years.

2. Reflection

When your grandkids leave your presence, what do they think about? Do you leave them thinking about anything? Reflection happens when a grandchild considers what you said or what they saw in your actions. Sometimes you may leave them with a question rather than always giving them the answers. Or it may be a statement given, not to show what a gray-headed stud you are, but to provoke their thinking.

Look, I believe most of your grandkids have grown up in a world where the seeds of truth have been scattered throughout their life. When they reach their teen years, you need to scale back on planting and spend more time cultivating. Cultivation includes turning the soil, adding fertilizer, watering, providing light, and sometimes pulling weeds. All these actions have a way of disrupting (in a good way) the landscape of your grandchild's heart to get them to internalize what they have been taught. Cultivation can move them out of dormancy into productivity.

Encouraging reflection is a way of engaging your grandchildren to take responsibility for their thinking and process life in a way that moves them on to emotional and spiritual maturity.

Try this. The next time you see one of your grandkids, find a quiet time to share with them. Tell them, "There's nothing you can do to make me love you more, and there's nothing you can do to make me love you less." It's a powerful statement that lets them know of your undying love for them, and it also gets them to think about your relationship. Teens know people love them when they're doing well; I'm not sure they believe that to be true when they're not.

Shift the way you engage with your grandkids, and you'll shift their desire from wanting just dollars from you to wanting more, something they can't get anywhere else.

3. Experience

I used to think if I didn't pray at the table before a meal or have a devotion at some opportune time or say something spiritual at the right moment, my kids or grandkids would never get to see the deep love I have for God or experience the joy I have because of a relationship with Him. I don't think that anymore.

I now believe the experiences we share together have an amazing way of communicating not only what I do, but also who I am. Let me repeat this again. The emotions of a lifetime are often found in the all-but-forgotten experiences of adolescence. It's an important statement.

I do believe as we hide God's Word in our heart, memorize His truth, and internalize His love for us, the expression of Him comes out at the most unexpected times. It sometimes comes out in the form of laughter. Or it is articulated in a discussion that doesn't fall back on *Christianese* but is principled on truth. It can be communicated through conversations that toss in golden nuggets of truth and wisdom that can only come from God Himself. Or it can be uttered in the most amazing and surprising locations and situations where we least expect it.

At this point, your actions do speak louder than your words. As you experience travel, meals, special occasions, vacations, funerals, weddings, and plenty of normal interactions, God will allow His Word to become flesh through you.

Spend more time lining up experiences than giving things that are one day going to rot, get destroyed, or become outdated. Buy a boat or a WaveRunner. Get that house at the lake. Buy a new grill for your patio and grill the greatest meals of all time. Go on a hunting trip. Take a trip to New York with your granddaughters. Go to concerts. Attend the Country Music Awards. Take a trip to the Grand Canyon. Go skiing (water or snow). Take a trip to the beach. Plan things that include your grandkids.

I owned a Harley and realized it was something my grandkids couldn't do with me. I see grandparents purchasing RV's and leaving their family behind to travel the country. I see other grandparents retiring and moving to where they can do what they've always wanted to do. They take up hobbies that don't include the grandkids. There's nothing wrong with any of these, but I would encourage you to plan and create experiences often with your grandchildren. They should know their grandparents aren't just people who have fun but are people who are fun to be with because of the shared experiences grandparents and grandchildren enjoy together.

Wisdom can be found in the lives of grandparents who have a wealth of insight and understanding, but it can only be imparted if those grandparents create an environment for their grandkids to discover it in them. Love means sometimes giving up your right to your own fun in order to show love by having fun with your teen grandchildren. I promise it's worth every bit of the sacrifice to leave a legacy of love.

CHAPTER 7

Understanding Your Teen's Behavior

Do not let wisdom and understanding out of your sight, preserve sound judgment and discretion; they will be life for you, an ornament to grace your neck. Then you will go on your way in safety, and your foot will not stumble. When you lie down, you will not be afraid; when you lie down, your sleep will be sweet.

Proverbs 3:21-24

It was a stormy, rainy, dark-clouded, thunder-filled day. And that was also the "climate" inside my office as I met with one of the angriest young ladies I had ever encountered. Every question I posed was met with a lightning-quick bolt of stinging, barbed words. The momentary sounds of silence were pierced by the thunderous retorts of a young lady who was mad at everything, and who had grown accustomed to "raining on anyone's parade." The Texas weather outside my office was exactly the same.

Bri exploded, and out of nowhere came a tornadic response, which bolted her from her chair. She headed for the door, cussing me out and yelling about how no one understood her. I quickly followed her out the door into the pouring rain of a Texas "frog-choker" of a storm. A bolt of lightning stunned her to stop and turn to look at me (now both looking like drowned rats in the sheets of rain). That's when I asked her…*what do you want*? I said it rather loudly, probably out of frustration and not knowing what else to say.

I told her the following: "You push people away. Everything you do is offensive. You're the angriest person I have ever met, and no one on this property (we have sixty kids that live with us) can stand to be in your presence. And no one knows how to help you, sweetheart. *What do you want*?" I didn't just tell her; I let her hear my feelings of defeat in a way that was way louder than the crack of any thunderbolt. My question was more about my defeat than it was about me having all the answers to help her.

We were both tired. She was tired of being angry and pushing people away from her. I was weary that nothing I was trying was working in my efforts to help her get to a better place in life. And we were both wet. Not just damp, but soaked to the bone! She looked at me with tears and raindrops streaming down her face, and it was then when I realized that God had placed this young "little punk" in my life to teach me a lesson about behavior. Everything turned into slow motion as she began to speak. And she said this…in a rather loud and aggressive way…

"I'll tell you what I want! I want you to love me the most when I deserve it the least!"

I didn't know what to say. In an instant, I realized I was completely missing her heart. I was so totally focused on her behavior that I forgot about her heart. This young lady was telling me her true need when all I was doing was trying to control her behavior and get her to quit doing things I found bothersome or offensive to others. And all the while, I was missing what was most important.

My first words came out easy, but they were not words I was used to saying.

"I am so sorry. I've completely missed it with you, Bri." It wasn't said in a loud voice. It was said as I slowly wrapped her in my arms, as the Texas rain ran down my butt crack. We were both soaked. And now more than ever, the streams of tears running down both of our cheeks soaked us. But I was also being soaked in something that rarely was displayed to "rebellious little snots" who are entitled, selfish, and *me-absorbed*. I was being soaked in grace—the offering of something when it is least deserved! And her heart was soaking it up like a dry sponge that prays for a Texas storm to fill its empty and parched holes.

Bri taught me a lesson. The behavior we all saw wasn't necessarily a reflection of who she really was. It was an expression of something else going on in her life, and I totally missed it.

All behavior is goal oriented. Behavior is a visible expression of the invisible issues. Behavior may be the warning lights on the dash of your car that says, "Hey, we've got a problem!" Behavior may be a scream for someone to notice when no one is paying attention. Behavior may be inappropriate actions rooted in a genuine need to fulfill a void or a heartfelt desire for value, love, and recognition.

> Behavior may be inappropriate actions rooted in a genuine need to fulfill a void or a heartfelt desire for value, love, and recognition.

One of the hardest tasks of any parent is to look beyond the behavior. I have learned the way to do this is to see with the eyes of my heart, not the ones on either side of my big nose. When you sit back and watch the behavior, rather than reacting to the rebelliousness or poor choices, you begin to realize there's a lot more going on than meets the eye.

I am not saying there shouldn't be consequences for violating the rules and boundaries you have established in your home. I believe in strong consequences and harsh "attention getters" that let children know how their destructive behavior and infringement on family values will not be tolerated. Consequences give power to the rules you have set. Those must be in place within your family.

Let your teens know there are consequences for some choices, but also let them know you'd like to discuss what's driving the behavior.

So, what are some of those drivers of your children's behavior? Why do they *do* what they *do*? What is their *motivation*? How did they decide to do what they did?

Again, I would caution you to not only apply these questions to the inappropriate behavior you see, but also to the appropriate and acceptable behavior. Why? Because I've seen just as many kids who seemingly "had it together" commit suicide as those who were a complete mess. The common theme I see with so many kids—good or bad—who either explode or implode, is parents who have a tough time getting to the core issues of their child's *heart-drivers*.

Here are five drivers that may be the motive behind the behaviors you see:

1. Loss

Loss is a simple concept, yet sometimes hard to understand. Loss is a void created in the heart of anyone, according to his or her perception. Allow me to give some examples of some teens' concepts of loss.

Loss is something that was and now isn't. It's the young lady who was a cheerleader and very popular in her earlier years, and for whatever reason, has now fallen out of that position with her peers. That loss creates a void in her life, which will now be filled in other ways. It's the same with a young man who was once athletic and has had an injury and can no longer be as active. Whatever he received from his athleticism (recognition, value, accomplishment, prestige, popularity) is now non-existent, and he will find new ways to get the same elsewhere.

Loss is a feeling for something hoped for, which didn't materialize. Maybe it's the hope for a boyfriend that never occurred or the position on a team that never happened. It is something that was anticipated and just didn't come about or an expectation that was never fulfilled. Loss isn't limited to what happened. Sometimes it's more about the death of what someone hoped would happen—like getting asked to a prom, being offered a chance at joining a fraternity or sorority, or a hope for an engagement, which didn't have a "ring" to it.

Many times loss is something that was and now just isn't. People experience this during the holiday season after the loss of a loved one. That person who was once there, no longer is, and a void is created. Many times, a loss is created when emptiness has been filled and then taken away. That loss, or feeling of emptiness, is where hopelessness enters the scenario and sleepless nights are consumed with unanswerable mind games, which pursue solutions to fill the newly created void.

Instead of just looking at their behavior, a parent must go deeper and look intently at the motivation of the behavior.

Loss is sometimes wrapped up in perspectives that if life would have been just a little different, then we wouldn't be in the position we are. It's the should-of, could-of, and would-of excuses that paralyze forward movement and forbid hope from entering the story.

Loss can also be victimization when someone has been violated, had something taken away or stolen, or stuck at the same stage of a traumatic happening.

An understanding of loss is critical to an empathetic, thoughtful, and considerate heart if parents want to be able to recognize a loss in the life of their teen. Instead of just looking at their behavior, a parent must go deeper and look intently at the motivation of the behavior.

The young lady acting out sexually might just be doing so because she has a desire (which is God-given) to feel valued. Her motivation is well founded; we all want to be valued. Her actions are inappropriate, but the drive behind it all may just be that she's never felt valued by those whom she lives with. Hear what I'm saying? As a parent, your focus will likely be to zero in on her sexual behavior, when the real issue may be that you have missed the opportunity to make her feel valued by you. It's the story of the speck and the plank. The speck in her eye is her sexual behavior. The plank in your eye is that you might have failed in making her feel valued, in the way *she* feels valued.

Here's another scenario. A young man who has never been able to become a man because of his over-controlling parents might just resort to physically fighting to express his manhood. Every young male wants to become a man. A parent's role is to help make this happen. But, while one is distracted by the teen's behavior, an examination for the losses in his life (the pursuit of manhood) must also be checked.

Now would be a good time to address this issue. We all miss one another. Don't think for a minute that you have been the perfect parent and never missed the heart of your child. We all do! That's not an excuse, but it is a reality. Your involvement in the lives of your children just might be a part of why they behave the way they do. You *are* a part of the equation.

The whole discussion about being genuine and authentic with your teens, a concept I push to every parent, is predicated on the understanding that your own imperfections will show themselves in your parenting. You won't get it perfect, and parenting never happens without us *all* missing the hearts of our teens. However, what a great place to start having a very real relationship of depth, as you get to the heart of all the issues that you and your teen wrestle with.

Here are some other heart drivers.

2. Performance for Acceptance

Teens want to be accepted. They long to have attention. It's a longing to be valued and appreciated. Don't we all want that? Sure we do. It's because God has created us all to be relational. And when some teens can't find it in certain permissible and acceptable ways (athletics, economic standing, academics, appearance, social skills, etc.), many move to socially unacceptable behaviors to gain attention. The young man that smokes pot, acts like a clown, shoplifts, or attaches his identity to some crazy group, may just be crying (and sometimes screaming) for acceptance; something every young teen desires.

3. Appearance

I recently sat at a restaurant in Mexico (on one of our trips to Cabo) and watched a young lady take close to one-hundred shots of herself posing in any way possible (with her parents at the table), trying to get just the right look to send out to her social networking site.

In a world where adolescent relationships are somewhat shallow, the need to appear "just right" becomes of utmost importance. It's really no different from you and me. When I go to a place to speak where no one knows me, I am more concerned about how I look than when I am to be around people who know me well.

I'm never surprised when a young lady sends nude pictures of herself to guys just to get someone to pay attention to her. It's the cathedral apex of a desire to be noticed, coupled with a teen's world

In a world where adolescent relationships are somewhat shallow, the need to appear "just right" becomes of utmost importance.

of shallow relationships, where every teen carries a camera. It's a scream communicating, "Look at me! Will someone just pay attention to me?"

4. Masking and Avoidance

Sometimes teens just want to avoid their past or mask the feelings that always seem to bubble to the surface. It's the young man who smokes pot to make himself feel different or forget the sexual abuse that occurred at a young age.

It's the young lady who will never dive deeper into conversations for fear that her close proximity to vulnerability might expose something she doesn't have the skills to resolve or talk about.

Kids run and hide for a reason. They avoid things for a reason. Here's a word to the wise: Teens usually avoid topics and discussions where they are shamed for expressing their opinions or observations. This shaming only pushes them to keep quiet, with the realization that it may just be better to "keep my mouth shut," rather than express feelings that might get "shot down" or ridiculed.

5. Anger and Vengeance

Anger is an emotional response to not getting what you want. Anger drives people to do crazy things. Their mindset takes on the position: "If I can't have it, then others shouldn't either." Anger drives other emotions, and usually, it can only be tamed by a relationship that provides help and hope.

A teen that bullies others, or is continuously negative and disrespectful to others, is typically driven by the idea that things haven't quite turned out as he or she wanted. What these teens had hoped for just didn't happen. This can be in any arena—sports, academic pursuits, social interactions, economic position, or possessions.

Every behavior you see is a direct result of a hidden motivation, and the person acting out the behavior does not always understand it. Some teens have no idea why they do what they do. The challenge of parenting is to help them understand the motivation behind their behavior.

All Behavior is Goal Oriented

As I said earlier, all behavior is goal oriented. Behavior is the visible expression of the invisible issue lurking inside the heart of your teen. I'm not implying that whatever you see on the "outside" is indicative of something bad on the inside.

Good behaviors can be motivated by unresolved heart issues just as easily as inappropriate behaviors find stimulus in those same issues. Here's an example:

I swam competitively for thirteen years. My motivation? To find value. As I reflect on my childhood, I recognize that not much value ever came from those around me. As a matter of fact, it was quite the opposite. That absence of value set my life on a course to find value elsewhere. I found value in swimming, where hard work produced medals,

Behavior is the visible expression of the invisible issue lurking inside the heart of your teen.

trophies, and blue ribbons. It was a good behavior, motivated by an issue of not finding value from life in my younger years.

I also found value when I first took a girl out to a concert while we were in the ninth grade. We stuck together for six years before we married. Hindsight would indicate that this high school relationship was one based on my selfish desire to find value. Again, another good behavior rooted in my need for value.

Another area of my life where I grabbed all the value I could was through my hard work. I've always been a hard worker and perhaps motivated by the fact that peers and others valued me because of my propensity to "get the job done" and to do it well. My driving mindset was to measure that value in dollars.

I later came to understand that I was using people and opportunities to selfishly gain value. And when value was not to be had from those occasions and relationships, I would move on to where I could find more value. That would lead me to always have to be right, take correction hard, and even lie to present myself as a valuable person. None of those behaviors were good.

Both the good behaviors and the not-so-good behaviors were ingrained in my search for value, trying to fill a void in my life that ultimately could only be filled by God Himself. Even though I now realize how my selfish motivation created some pretty inappropriate behaviors, I think I'll always have the tendency to go on my "value journeys." Perhaps it will always be a struggle.

My point is this, knowing the heart of your teen is critical and of utmost importance to the deepening of your relationship. Many believe that only unacceptable behavior comes from unresolved heart issues. Not true. There's plenty of acceptable behavior that is entrenched in unresolved issues. Your job as a parent is to know the heart of your child, regardless of the acceptable or unacceptable behavior. It's only when you address the true heart issues that you'll be able to convince anyone of their need to find the only source of real value. Unresolved issues in their life may also motivate your child's acceptable and appropriate behavior.

Remember the young lady that I mentioned earlier…the one who acted out sexually to get value she never felt she received? Well, she could have just as easily taken up competitive sports or theatre—the more acceptable behaviors. But she still has a value issue.

CHAPTER 8

TMI; Not Enough Wisdom

Blessed is the one who finds wisdom, and the one who gets understanding, for the gain from her is better than gain from silver and her profit better than gold. She is more precious than jewels, and nothing you desire can compare with her. Long life is in her right hand; in her left hand are riches and honor. Her ways are ways of pleasantness, and all her paths are peace.

Proverbs 3:13-18

We live in an information world. I recently read an Internet article by David Russell Schilling, in an industry newsletter called *Industry Tap*. The title of the article was "Knowledge Doubling Every 12 months, Soon to Be Every 12 Hours." It was written in 2013, so I'm sure that we've passed the date he projected. He stated the following:

Fuller created the "Knowledge Doubling Curve;" he noticed that until 1900 human knowledge doubled approximately every century. By the end of World War II, knowledge was doubling every 25 years. Today things are not as simple as different types of knowledge have different rates of growth. For example, nanotechnology knowledge is doubling every two years and clinical knowledge every 18 months. But on average human knowledge is doubling every 13 months. According to IBM, the build out of the "internet of things" will lead to the doubling of knowledge every 12 hours.

I'm sure his point was targeted for those interested in cutting-edge technologies. That's not my point in this chapter. My focus is more about how we, as parents, relate to a generation of teens who have more information and technology at their fingertips than in any other generation in the history of mankind. Our teens have access to information, data, evidence, statistics, numbers, records, facts, figures, collections, and just about any other type of document in any file or library. More information is not their heart's desire and ultimate longing. Instead, they're longing to find sources of wisdom, so they can take all that they've learned through the years and determine *what* they should believe and *why* they should believe it.

I now have the opportunity to just "ask Siri" on my smartphone and receive just about any information I want. Why, I can even entertain myself for an hour just carrying on a conversation with Siri, if all I want is information. And when I get bored with her, I can always go to "Alexa," who is happy to fill me in on just about anything I need to know, as long as it is information.

Teens long to find sources of wisdom, so they can take all that they've learned and determine what they should believe and why they should believe it.

When you and I grew up, written information (codified information) doubled every thirteen years. It's now doubling every eleven hours, and it will double every two hours next year. In three years, it will double instantaneously.

I don't know about you, but I would venture to say that you get just as filled up with information as I do, and most times, to the point that I just want to "shut it down." I need a break. In a world of over eight hundred television channels (I grew up on only three channels when the rabbit ears and aluminum foil was placed just right.) and countless news sources, I am moved to just "turn it off" when "my cup runneth over" with constant and endless yapping and sharing of more information. If you're like me, I get overwhelmed by the amount of information bombarding me every day. I'm tired of all the criticism, the endless sharing of opinions, and self-consuming presentation of many bent on always promoting themselves and what they think.

I feel this as I click back and forth watching CNN, Headline News, Fox News, and other nightly newscasts. I just want to turn it off. I feel the same way when I get on Facebook. The overpowering amount of information about someone's dog dying, another child being placed in St. Jude's Hospital, a funeral of a mother, a birth of another, updates on family happenings, prayer requests, news of fires in California, updates on natural disasters, and the constant bullying and negative comments about politics is just too overwhelming for me. Many are good things to know, but sometimes, my head and heart just can't keep up the pace.

And here's the kicker that all should understand. You and I, as parents, have a way to escape. We create homes of rest. We get to choose our schedules. We have the opportunity to take a break. We can get away on vacations. We've learned how to "take a breather." Our teens haven't and can't. Their world is one of constant bombardment of information. Their social media interaction demands constant attention. Why else do you think they're always staring and pecking away at their phones?

This is what is happening to our teens. They're shutting down. And in the process of shutting down to stop the constant flow of information, they're missing out on what they really desire the most. Wisdom.

The opportunities and contact points for gathering wisdom have been all but eliminated from our teen's social stage. The wisdom desired usually comes from older people in a child's life, people who have observed much, reflected on life's happenings, and have experienced more than those who are younger. It is from that wisdom that comes the principles of right living, insight, perspective, and discernment, which are all attributes for which our teens are desperately searching.

The intent of parents (and grandparents) to be fountains of information, when our sons and daughters are asking for something else, reminds me of the verse in Matthew 7:9 that states,

> *"Which of you, if your son asks for a bread, will give him a stone? Or, if he asks for a fish, will give him a snake?"*

A great concern that I have for this generation of teens is that they're beginning to view Scripture as just another source of information. And subsequently, ignoring it, because it is not conveyed along with an understanding of *why* it is so important.

When they ask for wisdom and you just give them more information, they look elsewhere for sustenance that will help them apply what they have learned. If you are just a source of information for your teens, they will shut you down, turn you off, and look elsewhere. What they're looking for is *wisdom*—how to take the principles and values they've been taught by you and apply them to the culture in which they live.

Sharing of information was needed and demanded in your child's earlier years when your role was one of a teacher. But now, as your child moves out of their childhood and into the world of adolescence, your role moves from a teaching role to a training role. They want something a little more than "learning more," and now desire to know the "whys" and "hows" and the purposes in what they have learned.

No one else has as much influence on your teen, nor do they have the access to them that you do.

My hope is that you will be the one who provides that wisdom for them, as no one else has as much influence, nor the access that you do. You can do this by switching your mode from teaching information-based values, to training wisdom-based concepts. This happens when you give the reason and meaning behind so much of the teaching that you have presented to your child in the first twelve years of life.

Here are a couple of examples.

I believe that teens view the biblical mandate of not having sex before marriage as just another piece of information. I can tell kids to "not have sex" a million times, but in this permissive world of information, they will ignore the truth within Scripture, unless they understand the *real* purpose of *why* God would desire for them not to do so. This is how I would transfer the wisdom behind the mandate not to have sex before marriage, so they can have a greater understanding of *why* I think this is important.

> Hey, you and I both know what Scripture says about pre-marital sex. But this is what I've seen and thought about for years. I've seen great couples lose their relationship, which should have lasted for years, because they "jumped the gun" and violated some good instruction. The reason God, who created you to be relational, would desire for you not to have sex before marriage is because He wants your relationship to last. Sex before marriage complicates relationships. It's your choice, but be careful if you want to keep from complicating this relationship you cherish. Don't risk it!

See the difference? My response is not just giving more information but sharing with them what I have observed, reflected upon, and experienced. It's sharing the wisdom behind the teaching.

If you want to have a discussion with your teen and battle over marijuana by just sharing information, and they're trying to justify their peer-accepted behavior, you're going to lose. That's what I've found out, especially when teens want to argue about which is worse—alcohol or marijuana?

There is plenty of research out there that would "informationally" (is that a word?) support their comments that alcohol is more detrimental to one's life than cannabis. In the information world, some teens will be able to quote the numbers of those who have died from alcohol abuse, versus those who have died because of marijuana use. If you do the information battle, you're going to lose.

Don't battle with information. Battle with wisdom. This is what I tell kids who always come to me with the targeted battle on their hearts. Here's an example:

> Look, I'm not going to argue with you about whether it's right or wrong to consume marijuana. I'm sure that much of what you say is accurate, and I'm sure that marijuana will one day be more and more permissible in society. But this is what I've seen, experienced, and thought about for years. I'm as opposed to you smoking weed to get through your day, as much as I am by your teacher at school having a glass of wine before he/she engages with students throughout the day. I've seen that marijuana has an amazing way of eliminating motivation and providing a way to escape challenges, rather than helping people learn the skills necessary to get through those challenges.

Neither of these discussions are arguments. They are opportunities to share what I have observed, reflected upon, or experienced, and how I have gathered wisdom in my life. People always ask me how they can get wisdom. This is what I tell them: You can get it by reflecting upon your experiences in life and by searching for the answers to the questions you have about the many challenges you've faced in your years on this earth. You can share your mistakes, struggles, and hardships, which you have encountered, and share the beauty of what you have learned through perseverance and persistence.

Pray. James 1:15 states, *"If anyone of you lacks wisdom, you should ask God, who gives generously to all without finding fault, and it will be given to you."* There are many times when I know I am meeting with a teen that I just say, "Okay, Lord, these have got to be your words…bring them to me at the right time."

You can listen. Listen to the heart of what your teen is really saying. And do this: Get counsel. Proverbs 26:16 whispers truth when we read,

A fool is wiser in his own eyes than seven people who answer discreetly.

Ask others. Benefit from their experiences and what they've contemplated through the years.

CHAPTER 9

Being a Superhero When Their Lives Suck

My message and my preaching were not with wise and persuasive words, but with a demonstration of the Spirit's power, so that your faith might not rest on human wisdom, but on God's power.

1 Corinthians 2:4-5

When my granddaughter Maile was sixteen, she texted me one time, "Poppa, can we get together for dinner? Just us?" I quickly responded that as soon as I got back in town from a speaking event, I would pick her up and we'd go wherever she wanted to eat. "Yes, Sweetheart, in a heartbeat," I replied.

You know what? She just wanted to talk. Not really about anything remarkable or astounding. That wasn't her point. She was really asking, *Am I valuable and important enough that you'd like to get together?* I heard it loud and clear and quickly responded, "yes."

One of these days, she'll ask if we can get together again, and it will be something remarkable, maybe earth-shattering. I'm convinced those critical conversations will never occur unless I'm willing to invest time in the smaller conversations that build trust and affection first.

Many times a grandparent is just the attending ear that listens and listens and listens and listens. When you're through listening, you listen a bit more. Somewhere in the midst of wearing your ears out, a grandchild begins to believe you're a superhero. All because you showed up and engaged in the nick of time. It's no different for any parent.

They'll remember your stories and bits of wisdom, just as you and I did growing up from the adults who spoke to us and into us. From my early childhood up through my thirties, I was like a sponge soaking up anything I could to figure out who I was, what I was supposed to do, and what my purpose was in life. It might not have taken me so long if the voices I heard in my elementary and teen years encouraged more than discouraged. My sponge soaked up quite a bit of negative from people who were more critical than wise.

Even after I became an adult, many other adults I knew spent time telling me what I couldn't do rather than what great things might be in store for my wife, Jan, and me. People said I shouldn't have dated Jan as long as I did. Some said we shouldn't have gotten married so early. We've now been married forty-two years. Some folks close to me said I shouldn't work for a church. I worked on a church staff for seven years. I met many parents who thought I was constantly wrong. In fact, I couldn't do anything right in their eyes. Many said moving to Branson, Missouri, to work for Young Life was a mistake. We spent seven years at YL as well.

The biggest punch in the gut was when a fellow sat with me and told me he didn't think I was capable of starting Heartlight. He thought it would fail if I tried it. He thought moving to Texas was going to be a big mistake, and he stated that I just wasn't capable of the plans I thought God had for us. In a way, he was right. I wasn't capable, but God was. He knew my calling, my passion, and my purpose. He created me for it. And it was His "positive push" that countered this man's negativity.

The people described were naysayers, people that always saw the glass half-empty and who took one-way trips to Negative Town, always emphasizing the worst of any situation.

I've said for years that it's not the presence of negative comments but the absence of positive comments that set one's life on its course. The positive for me came from older folks in my life who chose to sit with me and listen. All times of the day, any day of the week, they could be counted on to listen to my hopes and dreams, offering input only when I wanted it or asked for it. From them, I learned some important lessons that came from their ability to use experience and knowledge to make good decisions and judgments. Wisdom flowed from conversations. I'm sure they never realized the impact they were having on me. As I reflect on their effect on me, I guess their influence was what a grandparent could have offered me.

I've spent a lot of time looking back on my life, thinking about those people who helped me become who I am. As I try to imagine what I would be without their words of wisdom, well, I just can't. Most of these guys are dead now. Some have lost their spouse. Others have lost their mind. I still keep in touch with a few. All of their legacies live on in me.

When I worked as a youth pastor at the church in Tulsa, a fellow named Dave Tillack told me, "Mark, don't stoop to be a king when you're called to be a servant." Think about that one. For me, that was a totally different perspective than being told to put others ahead of myself—the same principle, but a new way of hearing and perceiving it.

The pastor of that church, Dr. L.D. Thomas, and I were out for lunch at the Tulsa Oil Club one time, and I remember him pointing to everyone in the room, saying, "Mark, every person in this room feels like they're carrying the weight of the world on their shoulders." Another pastor there, Doug Burr, told me a number of times, "Mark, God's going to use you."

I remember the renowned author and speaker Chuck Swindoll saying, "Everything that has come to you has first passed through the hands of God."

John Roberts, a swim coach I had for a number of years, said, "Mark, if you think you can, you will. If you think you can't, you won't. For many, a race was lost before the gun even sounded."

Smith Brookhart, a dear friend in Branson, Missouri, would remind me, "Markus, you're doing a good thing."

Spike White of Kanakuk Kamp, who took me under his wing, would say, "Mark, have you thanked the guy who fired you and brought you to Texas?"

Pete Herschend, another dear Branson friend, would say as we started Heartlight, "Mark, remember that your revenues will always be half of what you expect, and your expenses will be twice the amount you planned for."

Wishard Lemons told me when talking about ministry, "Mark, people in ministry don't laugh enough."

Joe Mooberry once said, "Mark, most Christian ministries cater to women; it's our job to serve up a good meal to men."

Cliff Taulbert shared with me over coffee, "Mark, you've got to be genuine, and you've got to be real, or people won't stand to be around you."

A lady named Margo Dewkett, who taught me about breaking horses, said, "Mark, how you treat a horse when you're on its back is pretty much how you treat those people that live around you."

All of these folks probably don't even know the impact each simple-but-wise sentence had on me. I'm not sure I knew how important they were at the time. In hindsight, I see how each molded me and how God used them to influence me. It was these guys (and gal) that left a legacy of hope for me. To each, I am most grateful.

It's interesting how each of the comments I remember these superheroes of mine making, didn't use Scripture. However, each undoubtedly stood on biblical principles for their own lives. Sometimes, wisdom is shared from the ways you have internalized God's Word in your life. You naturally express it through golden statements based on your experience and knowledge.

In all their time with me, each of these people had similarities in their influence that presented a wonderful example to me. Now I can use my influence, in the same way, to share wisdom with my grandchildren. You can too. There are a few common practices to note:

1. These one-liners didn't come out of just one meeting. They were nuggets I remember from a span of time we spent together. Conversations didn't set out to solve a specific problem at a specific time. They were just ongoing conversations over a long period of time.

2. These friends were intentional about training me. These meetings weren't just to shoot the breeze or pass time. They recognized they had a sponge sitting there, soaking up anything it could. They were purposeful (not agenda-driven), with a desire to pass on something that would make my life different.

3. Time spent together was positive. At least, it seemed like it was. I'm sure they said things that needed to be said, but I always left our times together with a sense of encouragement, not discouragement.

4. Each gave room for me to ask questions, millions of them. They weren't afraid to tell me answers I didn't want to hear, but they told them in an affirming way. I trusted them when they were right; I trusted them when they were wrong.

5. These steadfast rocks had insight, meaning they processed their own experiences and drew out insight and wisdom to be passed on to others.

6. They told stories. Their own stories of successes and failures, challenges and hurdles, and what they had learned or picked up in the process.

7. No matter how I saw something, each always helped me see things from another perspective.

8. Deep down, I knew each of these folks loved me and enjoyed the time we were able to spend together. I felt their commitment when they introduced me to friends, other colleagues, and folks we would bump into during our times together.

9. They didn't spend time correcting me by telling me how I needed to do something different, now or next time. If they did, I think I would have checked out and put them in the same category as other naysayers in my life.

10. They acted as a remedy, helping me figure out God's best for my life.

I'm sure you can list a very similar group of people that influenced your life. I bet you can list what each person taught you. Well, now it's your turn to be that influencer, storyteller, perspective-giver, sharer of successes, communicator of failures, insight injector, and positive trainer. God placed your child in your life for a reason. He also kept you in theirs for a greater purpose.

You've had plenty of years to have the light shine on you. Now it's their turn.

CHAPTER  10

How a Place of Retreat
Becomes a Haven of Rest

Come to me, all you who are weary and burdened, and I will
give you rest. Take my yoke upon you and learn from me, for I
am gentle and humble in heart, and you will find rest for your
souls. For my yoke is easy and my burden is light.

Matthew 11:28-30

Recently, I sat in a living room with a crowd of people who had come to see two older folks—grandparents who had gotten up there in years (each in their nineties). Four teens were in the room and some fifty-something siblings. Everyone listened as these two oldsters told all their medical stories of the previous six months. We all heard about hemorrhoids, calluses, bunions, bum knees, poor eyesight, hearing loss, something getting burned off, urine samples, and the need for another colonoscopy, endoscopy, and polyp removal. Getting old is not for the faint of heart.

I sat there trying to figure out how I could find a fork somewhere in the house and give myself a root canal to make the whole experience a little bit more pleasant. The four teens didn't utter a word. They were speechless after hearing all the graphic talk about the various health challenges. The rest of us periodically nodded and said, "Uh-huh," "Okay," and, "Then what did the doctor say?"

It was two hours of misery and gloom. As I suffered through it, I couldn't wait to get out of there and away from the discussion I really had no interest in. Am I exaggerating here? Maybe just a bit, but not far from the reality of that scene.

We may all be in that position one day when medical issues are about all we have to talk about. (I hope that day is a long way away.) I left thinking I never wanted my grandkids to feel as uncomfortable around me in my home as those teens did sitting around listening to the shocking realities of getting old. Then I started thinking, do I make some people feel just as uncomfortable in other ways?

My grandkids tell me I'm always cleaning. My daughter tells me I need to learn how to relax with messiness at my home. My son-in-law tells me that I can't always have everything perfectly put away. My wife says I'm obsessive-compulsive. You know what? They're all correct in their assessments. I can make anyone feel uncomfortable because there is something in me that always cleans. Always.

Guests become paranoid about whether or not they've put their dishes or cups in the right place, and family is always concerned I'm watching to make sure everything is properly stowed. If someone is missing something, they come to me first. They know I've probably thrown it away if it was just sitting around.

I have to work hard to keep my need for cleaning and picking up clutter from getting in the way of relationships within my family. I can only imagine how many times my kids and grandkids have looked for one of their belongings because they put it in the wrong place. Well, to me it was the wrong place. So I felt compelled to move it to the right place. They had to get used to my idiosyncrasies.

Jesus said, "Come to me all who are weary and heavy laden and you will find *rest*." He didn't say, "Come to me and you will find a way to give yourself a root canal." He said *rest*. I can't think of any group of people who deserve a place to rest, a place of sanctuary, more than your kids. They go out and do battle every day against a world that works against what they and we desire for their lives. They fight a contrary culture trying to steal their morals, values, faith, relationships, health, and peers. The least we can do is give them a place to recharge.

Our kids are looking for a safe harbor amidst the storm where they can refuel and be understood.

They're worn out. They're beat. They need a break. They need some rest. They need a retreat. They need a place where they are heard and listened to. They need a respite that refreshes and invigorates. They are looking for a safe harbor amidst the storm where they can refuel and be understood. I hope your kids find that in their own home. I hope you do too.

Let me ask you something. What do your kids feel when they walk in the front door of their home? Is it a place where they find the rest they need, or is it a place where they are more worn out by the time they leave? Do they tell each other stories behind your back, quietly making fun of the way you do things? Is it a place of avoidance where you know everyone will only get along if there is no talk of politics or religion?

Will they bring their friends to meet you? What do they sense from you? Do they feel welcome? Is there always an open invitation? Would they spend the night with you? Do they sometimes just want to hang out with their grandparents?

There are a number of ways your home can provide a setting for physical, emotional, and spiritual rest. These include the setting you design, the atmosphere you create, the rules of operation, and the conversations your home invites. Let me explain.

Setting

I bet your kids would love to come to your home and find a place warm in relationship, relaxed in its furnishings, and welcoming to every weary and heavy-laden teen. Like a favorite restaurant, they long for a place where they can be catered to, if you will.

I've walked into many a home where everything was in such order and so clean that it made me look messy! These homes feel like sterile environments that couldn't possibly allow the smallest amount of dirt or mess—whether it's physical or spiritual—to enter its doors. No controversial or messy talk would be found there. For teens, the welcome mat might as well say, "Don't cross this threshold."

If your home is an extension of who you are, then what message is your home communicating to your kids?

I've walked into homes where families are so concerned about how everything looks on the outside that teens feel like their *dirty* insides better not come anywhere near it. Performance and appearance reign supreme. This kind of home is so concerned with how everything looks that little attention is paid to what's happening inside the heart. As long as kids look great on the outside, all is well, even if they're falling apart on the inside.

When they were young, you probably taught your kids to put away the games, toys, puzzles, and dolls they played with, right? You told them there is a place for everything and everything in its place, encouraged tidiness, and supported the 1880s phrase: *Cleanliness is next to godliness.* Admit it, did you ever tell your kids the myth that a messy room means you have an unorganized mind?

Are you still saying things like, "Square it away," "Straighten it up," "Keep it in order," and "Clean up your room"?

Well, if your home is an extension of who you are, then what message is your home communicating to your kids? What message are your words communicating? What phrases do you use the most with them? Are you sending a message that says they have to have their lives in order, put together, straightened up, clean, tidy, and everything in its place to be with you? Or do you give signals that you and your home are a safe harbor where your kids can be a mess, fall apart, and be less than altogether?

I think they prefer the latter because it offers a hand of hope. That kind of message says, "You can fall apart here; messes are welcome." Which message would appeal to your teen?

Hey, I know about cleaning and having everything in its place. Believe me. So I have to work hard to create a haven that welcomes anyone who is a little disheveled and in disarray. My wife has a pillow on our sofa that says it wonderfully, "A Beautiful Mess." She puts it there just to bug me, a hard-to-miss reminder for me to quit cleaning.

Atmosphere

The setting has more to do with the physical attributes of your home. The atmosphere has more to do with *you*. From the moment your kids come in through the front door to the time they leave, you create the atmosphere.

Jan and I own a timeshare in Cabo San Lucas, Mexico, where I am writing this book. It's our second home, a getaway from all the hustle and bustle of travel, speaking, and living with sixty high school kids. I love this place. I love the food. I love the activity. I love the beach. I love the people. I love it all, except for one thing—the way that they greet me within five minutes of getting out of the taxi. Someone inevitably asks when they can meet with me so they can sell me something or push their agenda on me. It grates me. It's not the way to start a relaxing time away from home.

When your kids walk in the door, who is the focus of attention? Their first interaction should not be about what you want or planned, it should be about them and what they want.

I'd like to suggest some ideas that might help create the atmosphere you want, and will help them engage in the setting you create in your home.

- Build a fire pit in your backyard and create a place for conversation (not lecture).

- Sit around a fireplace more.
- Get tickets to a concert that your kids would like to attend and take them.
- Have a few good jokes to tell around the dinner table that will bring some belly-laughs or tell some old stories that will bring people to tears.
- Get that larger flat screen television and purchase whatever is needed to play some video games.
- Get a trampoline and put it in your backyard (for them, not you).
- Get a golf cart for your kids to drive around.
- Have plenty of board games to invoke fun and conversation, not *bored games* hated by all.
- Work on a thousand-piece jigsaw puzzle of a picture they like.
- Cook the meals they want.
- Have a refrigerator full of their favorite foods.
- Get up early and have a wonderful breakfast awaiting them.

You might be saying to yourself, "Now, wait a minute, Mark. This is my home, and my kids are already selfish and entitled enough to have me do the catering dance, where it's all about them." I get it. But once your atmosphere changes, the rules are lined out, challenges are faced head-on, the model of teaching transfers to a training mode, everyone learns the roles of everyone in the home, and respect is restored, you'll find it easier to put their needs before yours and engage in such a way that is met with gratefulness.

Don't have your music, your TV shows, your schedule, your favorite food, and your plans for games take over. This time is not about you. Remember, you only have so much time with your kids until you either kick the bucket or their calendar gets full and de-emphasizes your role in their life. They will be leaving your home soon. (They're only teens at your home for five or six years.) You have one shot during the teen years as a mom or dad. Make it count!

Above all, create an atmosphere where they know they are safe. A good friend of mine reminds me every time I see him that Jan and I are safe in his home. That is such a relief. It permits us to be ourselves, speak what is on our hearts, and share any concern or frustration that may be on our minds. It's an atmosphere that can only be created through relationship.

Rules of Operation

Okay, so I know many of you have read this far and probably think I advocate letting the crazies run the asylum. Just put the kids in charge and everything will be fine. You may think I promote just letting the kids do whatever they want. Not at all. I believe in rules to construct the boundaries and limits, so all can function within a relational environment.

Teens need to understand what is allowed and what is not allowed in your home. These rules are necessary. You may even need to put up a small blackboard or sign that says, "House Rules." When expectations are clearly stated, they can be correctly met. Everyone knows what's going to get them in trouble and what won't. Kids can still make either good choices or bad choices at that point, but they should know beforehand the limits and the consequences. Talk them out so you don't get taken advantage of when you can't hear or see them, or when you fall asleep before they do.

Here are a few rules I would include in your list:

1. Everyone and everything will be treated with respect.
2. You are always welcome here. Anything illegal is not.
3. This home will be a safe place for all. Don't think you are the only one here.
4. Bedtime is midnight. House is locked. TV, tablets, cell phones, game systems, laptops, and any other electronic devices are off.
5. No use of cell phones during meal times; video games limited to one hour.

6. If your parents have different rules, we support and follow them unless they make an exception for your visit.

7. We will share anything with your parents we think might be dangerous to you or others.

8. We don't expect to be taken advantage of. We don't owe you anything, but we want to give you everything.

9. No rudeness, crudeness, or nudeness, and don't kick our dog.

10. We can talk about anything, just keep it courteous.

11. You must understand there is nothing you can do to make us love you more, and there is nothing you can do to make us love you less.

Conversations Your Home Invites

Technology doesn't solve problems or create deeper relationships, conversation does. Good meals, a welcoming atmosphere, and a relational setting all work together so you can have conversations that offer opportunities to share your wisdom and give hope to your kids.

Another shift in the way you should act is to allow a conversation that reveals the messiness of life—your life and theirs. You need to shift the focus from expecting excellence to allowing for failure. Welcome their imperfect selves, imperfect lives, and their imperfect teen world to integrate with yours. Stop resonating perfection. They are old enough now to know nothing and no one is perfect. Anyone who expects perfection is a hypocrite or a fake.

Remember, I mentioned earlier (Chapter 7) how a teen needs to be in the presence of imperfect people as they begin to realize and comprehend that their once-perfect world is just not anymore. Grasping this is tough. It's sad. And, yes, it's messy.

Making imperfection more comfortable is essential. "For all have sinned and fall short..." (Romans 3:23, KJV) now becomes a reality. Teens can more than relate to what Paul wrote to the Romans when he said, "For I do not do the good I want to do, but the evil I do not want to do—this I keep on doing" (Romans 7:19). This is not the time to be quoting to your teen, "Be perfect, therefore, as your heavenly Father is perfect" (Matthew 5:48). That will only discourage, not encourage.

Admitting imperfection is really pretty easy because you have never been perfect. No one is this side of heaven. Confession is the key. It makes you relatable to your teens. This should happen in the form of sharing stories of struggle, failure, disappointment, and hardship. Tell your kids when it was hard to forgive and easier to hate. Tell them how you handled it when someone picked on you. Tell them your biggest disappointments and what you later learned from them. Unfold the conversations at natural intervals, in short stories on walks, during games, in the car—not

A teen needs to be in the presence of imperfect people as they begin to realize and comprehend that their once-perfect world is just not anymore.

lecturing but doing life together. Your imperfect conversations are essential to open the door for them to talk about their newly discovered imperfections.

Your words affirm their struggle and give them hope that they, too, can overcome the struggles and difficulties they face in their teen years and beyond. Your words help them identify with you. Your shared experiences connect you.

A young father of four once told me after attending one of our seminars that the day his dad admitted failure and showed himself to be imperfect was the day hope was ushered into his life. I can tell you this for sure. Your teen children don't care as much about your accomplishments as your stories of disappointment. Your accomplishments may motivate; your stories bring hope. So be careful of your words and how you come across. The setting, the atmosphere, and the rules of your home create a pathway for a conversation that is open and raw, vulnerable, and bonding. In his 1960 book *The Four Loves*, author C.S. Lewis lamented the opposite of such an atmosphere in families at times and affirmed the power of positive words from parents and grandparents alike.

We hear a great deal about the rudeness of the rising generation. I am an oldster myself and might be expected to take the oldsters' side, but in fact, I have been far more impressed by the bad manners of parents to children than by those of children to parents. Who has not been the embarrassed guest at family meals where the father or mother treated their grown-up offspring with an incivility which, offered to any other young people, would simply have terminated the acquaintance? Dogmatic assertions on matters which the children understand and their elders don't, ruthless interruptions, flat contradictions, ridicule of things the young take seriously—sometimes of their religion or insulting references to their friends—all provide an easy answer to the questions, *Why are they always out? Why do they like every house better than their home? Who does not prefer civility to barbarism?* (Lewis, 42)

Your home must be a place of fun, hope, relaxation, and safe harbor for teens where they know your deep love for each of them.

Your home will one day be silent. The chaos of kids will be gone. Time moves on and so will your family. My hope for you is that everyone's memories of your home will be of rooms full of love, a kitchen overflowing with great scents, and walls that echo laughter. I hope your home is a place of fun, hope, relaxation, and safe harbor for teens that know that they know, that they know, your deep love for each of them.

CHAPTER 11

Touching Their Heart When Their Behavior Hurts Yours

And we know that God causes all things to work together for good to those who love God, to those who are called according to His purpose.

Romans 8:28 (NASB)

M y son's phone call was expected. His message was not.

"Dad, I'm getting divorced," he said. The neighbors could hear my response, I'm sure. "What do you mean, you're getting divorced? You just got married! What are you thinking?" "I've met someone else," my son said. I remember telling him, "Well, Adam, when you can call your wife's father and apologize for screwing up her life, then I'll talk to you." Doesn't that sound great? Wasn't it manly? I thought I was doing the right thing, standing up for what was right. I was defending what God desires and what we stood for as a family. I said that to my son as well. Mind you; this was the same son who inspired the tagline of truth I've communicated to hundreds of thousands of parents—*There's nothing you can do to make me love you more, and nothing you can do to make me love you less.* Now I wasn't so sure.

When my son needed me the most, I wasn't anywhere to be found. While he was lost, I let him wander. When he needed a dad who would walk with him through a difficult time, I wrote him off. And I did so all under the guise that I was doing what was right "in the eyes of the Lord." Quite honestly, I was so angry that I was really just trying to find some scriptural justification and excuse for my disappointment and rage, which was burning deep inside my heart. The understanding of imperfection is easy to wrap my brain around. The fact that it had come to display itself within my family was hard to swallow and choking out my image of what things were supposed to be like in a perfect world. My anger was because I was hurt by this breaking of an image of perfection that had a lot more to do about me than it did about my son.

During this difficult time, my presence in my son's life was lacking. Then I woke up one morning and realized what I thought I was doing in the name of righteousness wasn't working. The more I thought about it, the more I came to see how I put my expectations above my own son. I justified my behavior with the idealistic thoughts that I was doing what God wanted me to do. Boy, was I wrong.

Adam hurt me. When I turned my back on him, it was because of my own feelings. I was thinking more about myself, and how I was going to lose a daughter-in-law whom I loved, rather than my son's turmoil. I did not consider the internal conflict and struggle he was going through. Yep, I put myself first.

Just today I had a salesman tell me, "I like finding out where other people are wrong, and I love having them say I was right." His comment was exactly how I responded when my son hurt me. I've spent hours of reflection since then looking in the rearview mirror. I believe God would have me spend more time trying to touch the hearts of those who are hurting me than protect my own heart or convince myself I am protecting God's very own heart by turning my back on any one of His precious kids.

A father of one of the kids who lives with us recently let me know he was disappointed in me. I wasn't standing up to the media and publicity he felt were exploiting his daughter. She was engaged in a same-sex relationship, and the media loved revealing this scandal. The media exposure defamed him, his wife, and Heartlight. The media was relentless and started making accusations that our program was into *conversion therapy.* They tried to paint Heartlight as something we are not.

Eventually, I decided it would be best for this man's daughter to leave our program. It wasn't working for any of us. The media exposure portrayed Heartlight falsely, and we could not find a good resolution in the situation. I also thought that publicity could bring problems to other families and teens entrusted to us at that time.

This father and mother are dear people. They love their daughter immensely. Asking them to come pick her up from our program was hard on them and me, but the choice I had to make was in the best interest of the Heartlight program. The father caught me somewhat off guard when he said, "This approach is not what I would have expected. It gives the impression of fear, not confidence in the Lord's provision." He felt we should fight, not only for his daughter, but also against the homosexual agenda. I disagreed. That is not Heartlight's mission. I just didn't think that was our fight.

His comment got me thinking quite a bit about what stand we are supposed to take when we encounter people and situations that don't follow what we believe. Scripture says the following:

> *But you, man of God, flee from all this, and pursue righteousness, godliness, faith, love, endurance and gentleness.* Fight the good fight of the faith. *Take hold of the eternal life to which you were called when you made your good confession in the presence of many witnesses.* (1 Timothy 6:11-12, emphasis added)

I believe the fight mentioned here means fights and quarrels that get us caught up in arguing over things that create nothing eternal. Matter of fact, I further believe this Scripture is pretty targeted at encouraging people to fight the good fight that pursues righteousness, godliness, faith, love, endurance, and gentleness. All these things are eternal.

I don't think this Scripture means I am to fight everything that doesn't line up with God's Word. Hey, I'm not looking for a fight. The teens around me get beat up enough from peers. I don't want to look for a brawl in which there is always one winner because that also means there is a loser. I don't want to be a loser. I sure don't want any teen around me to think he is a loser either.

I also don't think this Scripture tells me I must fight other people's battles. Some people really believe it is their job to create or finish all fights. I don't. Some admirable and honorable battles just aren't my business. If I spend all my time trying to fix all the cultural and political issues around me, I doubt I would have any time to develop relationships. Love might get lost in the fight. I am called to love on people the way God directs me to do so. When I love on them correctly, and we develop relationships, then I can step into a fight for them or with them, rather than fighting against something. When that happens, we both win. There's nothing wrong with fighting for a cause. It's just that some of those causes aren't mine to fight.

So, where does this come into parenting?

You are getting older. You have things you believe in and a number of things you don't believe in. There are things in this world you don't agree with, and probably there are many things you downright despise.

As this new and changing culture emerges, don't confuse love and listening as acceptance. No one is saying you have to embrace what you believe is sin. It's just that sometimes (I would argue most times) we need to let the Holy Spirit be in charge of making those we love *accountable* for their sins. That's the Spirit's job anyway, isn't it? Who made it ours?

Be careful. It's easy to get caught up in some of the quarrels and controversies that are more about fighting than they are about resolution. Maybe the way you believe is different from the way your child believes.

You can spend the time fighting and lose the relationship, goodwill, and love. Or you can love in spite of the differences in your beliefs and still be able to listen and impart your stance without offense and without losing your special relationship.

Here's what the Bible states right before that verse about fighting the good fight:

> *They have an unhealthy interest in controversies and quarrels about words that result in envy, strife, malicious talk, evil suspicions and constant friction between people.* (1 Timothy 6:4-5)

My message is simple. Don't fight for something that produces nothing. Don't engage when it only produces anger and destroys relationships. Instead, fight for the relationship with that special person God has placed in your life when you encounter differences of opinions, no matter how big or small.

Don't fight for something that produces nothing.

Some situations may be hard to swallow, but they may also be the biggest opportunities to show how much you love your children in spite of your differences. I encourage you to think about these possibilities before you are faced with any of them, so you don't react negatively when you find out what's going on. Think about these now, so you can keep your head on straight if any of them occur within your precious family.

You have to figure out how you would respond when you first hear that your son or daughter is gay. You may have to accept (I said accept, not agree) the fact that your son is living with his girlfriend, and you'll have to figure out how to love him even if you don't approve of the living situation. You will probably have a child who thinks it is okay to smoke pot. Will you let the difference in how you feel about something that has no eternal value determine (or destroy) the relationship you have with your child? If you differ on politics, the changing climate, or same-sex marriage, do you think you can share wisdom about these hot topics when there is disagreement on the particulars?

Can you still participate and attend a child's wedding if the couple is already expecting a baby? Can a discussion about transgender bathrooms and same-sex marriages produce a perspective that your son or daughter has never seen before? Can you still love a son or daughter who sees nothing wrong with smoking, gambling, drinking, or other violations of your standards? Will your daughter still feel the specialness of the relationship with you if she is just a little immodest and parties more than you ever would have wanted? Can you continue to love your children if they marry people you don't like or approve of? Will you still be involved in their lives in a way that leaves the legacy God designed you to leave?

These scenarios are easy to read on the page, but much harder when they hit home. When any of these scenarios happen within *your* family, what will your reaction be? Hopefully, these situations are not just sprung on you, but are preceded by a few conversations and time for you to give wise (and sensitive) input when it counts the most. You have an opportunity to help form opinions and beliefs, rather than just being a recipient of your child's announcements or being a bystander, watching behavior you think is inappropriate.

Your words of encouragement can be a rudder that steers even the mightiest of ships to a different destination.

Your relationship is key. The God of relationships calls you to be a light in the darkness and a beacon of hope. Your words of encouragement can be a rudder that steers even the mightiest of ships to a different destination or a spark that lights up the darkest of nights.

You may think, *Okay, how do we do that, Mark? How do we approach a subject or situation that is contrary to what we believe without alienating our child? What do we say? Will our kids even listen to us?* Great questions.

First of all, yes, they will listen to you, but only if you have already established a solid relationship where you are a trusted source of wisdom. If you haven't built the relationship, then I doubt you can come in and share your opinion

Without relationship, giving unasked-for advice creates more distance.

and make much of a difference. Without relationship, giving unasked-for advice creates more distance. Chances are, your teen already knows what you believe regarding the situations I listed above. They are fighting mighty internal battles. They already fear disappointing you. They already worry you will condemn them.

If you won the right to be heard with your presence throughout their lives, then yes, I believe they will listen. Your approach to your teen at critical times shows what your relationship can withstand. However, what you say, and the tone you use, sets the course for ongoing input and interaction.

As your kids reach their teen years and beyond, when you need to talk about something tough, I'd approach the discussion by saying, "You and I know I'm older than you, and I don't see things in the same way that perhaps much of the world accepts. We're different, you and I, but we have had, and always will have, a special relationship. Right now, I want to speak to the *elephant in the room.* Tell me what's going on in your life. I want to know what you're thinking."

That should get you in the door to have the conversation. Remember to ask questions. Whatever the answer (however misguided in your eyes), ask more questions. Hopefully, after you spend a period of time of listening, your child will ask you something along the lines of, "What do you think?"

Be careful here. I find sometimes it just isn't a good idea to share your opinion. Many times I look at kids when they ask that question and say, "It really doesn't matter what I think. I'm happy for you, and you know I'll never let any of your decisions get in the way of our relationship."

There's a Scripture that states,

> *Fools have no interest in understanding; they only want to air their own opinions.* (Proverbs 18:2, NLT)

That reminds me to wait when I am asked for my opinion. I need to consider first, *am I being a fool? Do I want to understand my teens? Did I really hear their heart, or was I formulating my own counter arguments the whole time they shared?* Sometimes my opinion is just not needed. Other times, it may instill a sense of disappointment in my child.

Let me ask you this. Once you hit your teen years, didn't you know your own sin better than anyone? Did you hide things from parents or even trusted friends? If anyone *caught* you or *condemned* you for your choices, did it help? Most of the time, teens know exactly what they are doing wrong in their lives. In fact, often, they feel worse about themselves than they really are. They feel worse about their mistakes and failures than you could ever make them feel. If they are making poor choices in some areas and have been *brought up better*, then they most likely already think the ones they love see them as utter failures, not just human beings who mess up sometimes. They don't need to hear it. They need to be loved and encouraged through it.

That verse in Proverbs directs me at times to simply respond with, "I understand." They may say, "So you're okay with me doing (whatever it is they are doing)?" My response is, "I didn't say I agree with you. I said that I understand, and we can still love one another and not agree with everything you're doing."

If I sense my opinion or perspective will be ignored at that time, then I don't share it. That's like casting pearls before swine (not that I'm calling my kids pigs, although I'm chuckling on the inside as I write this). You know what? I can still wholeheartedly love and embrace a child who doesn't want or take my advice.

One big key to parenting is *don't take it personally*. After all you have tried to teach and instill in them, their sin and poor choices can certainly feel personal. When your children hurt themselves or damage their lives or the lives of others, of course, it hurts you. Sometimes it hurts bad. However, you can't make your hurt the focus, or you will lash out in ways that won't be welcome. Put your hurt feelings aside for now. You're the grown-up.

If you are reading into my comments asking if you are ever to "stand up" for what you believe, the answer is a resounding "Yes!" There are times. But there are also times that you embrace the fact that kids will hurt you along the way, and NOT allow that hurt to deter you from the love you share with them. It's called grace—moving toward your child when, in your mind, you have every right to walk the other way.

This chapter doesn't negate the great need to formulate and execute the rules and consequences needed for the operation of your home, which are based on beliefs you hold dear. Rules are important. And so is letting a child, at any age, know that they are loved where it would be easier not to.

Oh, and my son Adam? He married again, as did his ex-wife. He married a girl he loves dearly, and my ex-daughter-in-law married the man of her dreams. They both posted on Facebook the same day announcing the birth of their kids. Out of the thousands of Facebook friends I have, their posts were listed right underneath each other. What are the chances of that?

It was almost as if God was trying to tell me that regardless of circumstances, and regardless of whether I understand or even agree with them, He does work all things together for good. He uses pain to create passion and purpose. He makes your mess into your message. He takes tests and turns them into testimonies. He did it for my son and for me. I stand witness to how He does it for thousands of teens who spend time at Heartlight. You can trust He will do it for your children and you, no matter their age.

CHAPTER 12

Your Relationship With Your Teen

*I did not come with superiority of speech or of wisdom…I was
with you in weakness and in fear and in much trembling…*

1 Corinthians 2:1-3 (NASB)

I'm going to be asking a number of questions instead of giving you
just answers. My hope is to get you to review, question, and set a
new course with your family so that you can offer what is needed to your
teen.

Now, I'm simple in my approach. Many times, just asking questions
brings parents to the right conclusions. But if you're still stumped a bit and
feel a little confused, hold on. We still have a few more chapters to answer
those lingering questions.

If *reflection* is a source of wisdom, I hope you'll take this time to
reflect on yourself and embrace that, as culture changes and your teens
mature, you must transition your approach for engaging with your teens in
order to offer cultural relevance to timeless truth.

So, how is your relationship with your teen?

Good? Not so good?

Growing? Dying?

Flourishing? Failing?

Engaging? Disengaging?

Moving closer together? Moving further apart?

Connected? Disconnected?

Wherever you are on that spectrum, my hope is that each day that passes, you're moving closer together, even if you're in the midst of turmoil. A crisis has an amazing way of bringing out the worst in everyone. At the same time, I would tell you that a crisis possesses the opportunity to bring out the best in folks as well. I say this because I know that a crisis doesn't *just happen.* Chances are if you have a crisis in your family with your teen, it's been growing for a while, and the explosion you now see has been bubbling under the surface for a bit. Once the explosion is weathered, it is time to deal with what lies underneath—the true heart of the matter.

> Conflict is a true precursor to change.

Conflict is a true precursor to change. And if you want something different for your family, many times you must go through the tough stuff to get to the tender parts of the relationship. So, here are a few bits of wisdom that will hopefully help your relationship, whether you're in a crisis or calmness. These truths remain true regardless of the battle raging around them.

1. The most important relationship that your children can have during their adolescent years is with *you*!

I'm convinced of this. If you want to maintain that relationship, even if they're smoking pot, tell you they're gay, sexually active, hate the church, or hate you, you must move toward them relationally. I know this to be true. If you live with teens (and I have—thousands of them), you will be hurt by their comments, accusations, and decisions. No parent is immune. It's the process of your child growing up and learning to spread his/her wings. But in reality, the spreading of wings sometimes knocks over anything within their wingspan—including you.

It's about grace, even if they have or are hurting you.

Offering them something (your relationship) when they deserve it the least is one of the hardest roles a parent will ever play. Let me say something about grace here even though I've mentioned it earlier. It's hard to offer when you've been offended. Scripture tells us, "*A brother wronged is more unyielding than a fortified city; disputes are like the barred gates of the citadel*" (Proverbs 18:19). When your children offend you, it's hard to move back toward them. Grace moves you back into relationship, just as God has done for each of us.

If it's easy for you, it's probably not grace. True grace is tough! But not offered, it means that you can only love your child when he or she doesn't hurt you. Part of unconditional love is telling your child, "There is nothing you can do to make me love you less, and there is nothing you can do to make me love you more." This is easy to say, but hard to implement when your heart has been hurt.

Regardless of the hurt, your teens want a relationship with you, even when you (or they) can't see it. You'll never get to the relationship stuff if you move away. No battle has ever been won by running the other way.

I am reminded of what C.S. Lewis once said, "I don't doubt God's desire to want the best for us. I just wonder how painful it's going to be." I chuckle every time I see that quote because it is so true. The question that comes to my mind is, "Could God be using pain to show us the path back to a true relationship with our teen?" Could be.

2. If you have a discipline problem, you have a relationship problem.

I've said this a million times. You're going to have to figure out what is separating you from your child, or has the potential to do so in the

119

future. As stated earlier, the behavior you see is the visible expression of the invisible issues going on in the life of your teen.

Don't think the discipline issues that you have to deal with are just your teen's problem. If the inappropriate behavior is getting in the way of your relationship with your child, the problem may not be the behavior, but rather, the relationship you have with your teen. No teen is an island.

3. Teens change because of relationship, not the exertion of your authority.

An old-school thought about discipline was predicated on the fact that teens would respect authority, listen first to what their parents had to say, and do whatever their parents wanted them to do. Times have changed, haven't they?

Teens don't look at authority the way they used to. There are several reasons they don't, regardless of how you believe and what you desire for your family. Because of the many changes in an adolescent's social structure and perspective of the world, the only way to a teen's heart is through a relationship.

That doesn't mean that you don't desire respect, nor do you neglect the implications of disrespect. But it does mean that the "front door," which you used to come in through (i.e., the exertion of authority), won't gain you access to the "living room" of their life. You're going to have to change the way you enter, and that means choosing a different door. This doesn't mean that your front door approach is wrong. You're just not going to gain the entrance to the heart of your teen unless you enter through a different way.

Let me ask you this:

- Do you want things to change in your home?
  Look at your relationship.
- Do you fight more than you thought you would?
  Look at your relationship.

- Do you feel like you don't know your teen anymore?
  Look at your relationship.
- Is your teen disrespectful, disobedient, or dishonest?
  Look at your relationship.

4. There's only one person in this world that you can change... that's *you*.

So before you start looking at the speck in your teen's eye, look at the bigger plank in yours. I'm not saying there is nothing wrong with what your teen is doing. That needs to be dealt with, but the first step is to look at yourself.

That's the best place to start. It's time to take a personal inventory.

Let me ask you some more questions:

- Do you do things that provoke your teens?
- Are your interrogating skills more like a police investigator than a caring mother or father?
- Do you violate the privacy of a seventeen-year-old, who can serve in the military in a few months, just to check where they've been on the Internet?
- Do you exhibit anger problems when they make poor choices?
- Do you project your frustrations on them (when it's really more about you than them)?

Are your expectations for your teen creating a wall, rather than a path to walk through? Do you constantly correct, letting your teen know how to do it better or should do it differently next time? Things don't always have to be "great." It's okay for things just to be "good" sometimes. If not, you are creating a world of frustration for your teens, and they'll never be able to jump through all the hoops of *greatness* you expect. They'll eventually shut down.

Do you say things that bug your teen? Are you inappropriate at times? Do you post things on your social network accounts that would be better off left unsaid? Do your teens think the conflict is more about you than about them? Are you still treating your teen like he was ten or like she was still your little eight-year-old princess?

Have you missed some important things in the life of your teens? Has your *busyness* communicated that they're not valuable? What is the priority in your life...work or your teens? Have you made some mistakes which have been the cause of turmoil within your family? Affairs? Poor choices? Personal problems that need to be resolved? Habits you can't break? Are there some unresolved issues from when you

Are your expectations for your teen creating a wall, rather than a path to walk through?

were a teen yourself that you've never dealt with and they've now "come up" when you have a teen? Is there a lack of forgiveness toward your parents? Do you have negative feelings towards someone who has offended you, which tends to come up whenever you're angry? Feel like others have controlled you to such an extent that you'll never let anyone do that again, so you take total control of your teen's life?

Are you critical and sarcastic? Are discussions more about your opinions, rather than you listening? Do you move into discussions just so that you can share your opinion because no one else will listen? I ask all these questions just to stimulate some self-reflection, which might show your part in the crisis at home. It's hard to push a teen to resolve that which you have not. So here are a couple of issues that I think are found in most families. And these could be the same issues causing some of the problems you are facing.

Mom, can I give you a slap and a kiss? Here's the slap. You talk too much. You must quit talking to your teen at the same pace that you talked to them when they were in elementary and middle school. All your talking worked then, when you operated in a teaching mode, but it doesn't work when you transition into a training mode. Your incessant talking will shut your teens down, and they'll never have an opportunity to get a word in edgewise. They want to be heard, not have to hear about everything over and over and over. That's the slap, but here's the kiss. Every man knows this. One woman possesses more wisdom than all of the men reading this book. And if your constant talking shuts your teen down (wait for it!), they will never receive all the wisdom you have, which they so desperately need. They'll turn off the TV before they ever get to watch your program.

Remember this: Not every teachable moment needs to have a lesson tied to it. Not every discussion has to have a Scripture embedded in your wording. Sometimes you appear wise when you keep your mouth shut; even a fool appears wise when he keeps his mouth shut. Give it a try. Quit sharing so much information. Remember, they want wisdom, not more information. You'll be amazed at your teen's response.

Okay Dad, it's your turn. Quit trying to fix everything. I know we're made that way. We're supposed to fix things. And we let that carry over to our sons and daughters. The message they hear is that they have to be "fixed" or they won't be loved. Your teen is not a project to be fixed.

Every time I'm at a hotel or a guest at someone's home, it seems like I'm always cleaning out a drain,

> Not every teachable moment needs to have a lesson tied to it.

fixing a shower head, replacing light bulbs, or offering to fix something. Sometimes it's embarrassing to my hosts that I had to fix something because it reminds them of what they can't do or haven't done. So now I just fix things without ever telling them.

Remember these things, Dad. Not every conversation needs to have a conclusion. Look at it this way. There are times in which directives and comments need to happen to steer your teen's life along the right path. But most of the wisdom transferred will actually happen during the time you spend with your teens and the ongoing discussions you have, which might involve topics they'll deal with over the years, or even a lifetime.

As one who wants to influence the life of teens, I find that keeping my discussions open-ended allows for further and future discussions. This is the best way to have an ongoing relationship. Here's another piece of wisdom I've gathered from teens. It's okay for your teen to be undone, disheveled, and not all put together. When I engage with struggling teens and start the lifelong discussions, they learn that I care about them—as much when they're screwed up as when they have it all together.

Dad, your constant reminders that there is something broken with your teens (by trying to fix them all the time) needs to be countered with a presence that communicates you can still love your teens, in spite of their brokenness. (I'm sure they feel the same way we do as husbands when our wives tell us what is wrong with us. It pushes us away.)

Here's something for both moms and dads. It is best described by a short story about my daughter, Melissa Nelson, and her daughter, Macie, a twelve- (soon to be thirteen-) year-old.

Melissa was trying to help Macie with her schoolwork, pushing her to do her best, to get it right, and make good grades. Every parent wants that for his/her child, right? Well, Macie became frustrated at not getting it right all the time and hearing the constant good intentions of Melissa helping her. Macie stood up and said in a ridiculing and sarcastic way, "Hi, I'm Melissa Nelson, and I know everything!" Melissa took away her phone as a consequence of being disrespectful, but I've got to say, I think the story was rather hilarious when she told us what happened. Here's the lesson for all of us. No one likes a know-it-all. If someone knows it "all," there is no reason for him or her to have a relationship with anyone else.

Wow! Is that a lot of stepping on toes or what? I hope so. I want you to reflect on yourself and figure some things out, in order to prevent your child from rebelling against some of the things that just aren't right in your home.

As you work through this chapter (which I think is the most important

YOUR RELATIONSHIP WITH YOUR TEEN

one), I want you to know this. Listen to your spouse; they may be correct in some of their observations. Admit where you are wrong. And pray this prayer, "*Lord, search me, know my heart, test me and know my anxious thoughts...and see if there is any offensive way in me*" (Psalm 139:23, 34).

CHAPTER 13

Put Down the Phone;
Pick Up the Conversation

Listen to my cry, for I am in desperate need; rescue me from those who pursue me, for they are too strong for me.

Psalm 142:6

Hey, we're all busy. And we've all had our lives complicated and distracted by these new devices that have reshaped the way we all communicate and socialize. It's important that we not miss out on some pretty essential habits that connect us with our kids and deepen our relationship with them.

You've seen the same things I have. Restaurants are packed full of hungry patrons more interested in communicating with others not at the table than with those sitting across from them. Airplanes are full of travelers who would rather play angry birds or solitaire, rather than carry on a conversation with someone that is right next to them. Or how about the person texting friends as they speed sixty miles an hour down the highway, distracted from what is most important at the moment? Or teens, in any situation, who are stuck on their phone, communicating with their fingers, and not speaking to those in their presence. We're losing the opportunity to transfer concepts that our teens desperately need. And we're all missing opportunities because we're looking at a screen, rather than at what God may have just placed in front of us.

Hey, I know it's consuming. That's why I don't have any games on my phone. They are too much of a distraction for me. A few weeks ago, I was with an elderly couple whom I have known for forty years. They are both eighty-two years old. As I sat down, John said, "Mark, I just want you to know that we have a rule when we have dinner. The first person that picks up their phone has to pay the tab for the meal. And I want you to know that I always order a very expensive bottle of wine." I knew what he was saying. We didn't get together so that we could spend time with others. We came together so we could spend time with each other. I turned my phone off.

Here's a good question to start off this lesson. Why do you talk to your teen? It's a fair question, right? And the second question is this: Is your discussion with your teen more about you—your need to have a discussion, your desire to talk, and your need for information? Or are your conversations more about them—their heart and feelings? I had a mother tell me this past weekend, "I need to have conversations with my teen so I feel like I'm doing what I'm supposed to be doing." When I asked her, "Did you hear what you just said? It's clear to me that your conversations are more about you than they are about your child?"

In his book, *The Purpose Driven Life*, Rick Warren states it well in the first sentence of the book, "It's not about you!" In the early years of your child's life, talking and talking is effective, because you are in a teaching mode. But as teens move into adolescence, the purpose of discussion should shift and be more about them. Remember that verse in Scripture that says, "*Do nothing out of selfish ambition or empty pride, but in humility consider others more important than yourselves*" (Philippians 2:3)? This applies to conversations during the teen years as well. It's essential that you shift your purpose when talking, from one of sharing information to that of listening, if you want to touch the heart of your child.

Do you talk for these reasons?

- To show interest?
- To transfer wisdom?
- To encourage?
- To gain further understanding?
- To display affection and love?

What would your teen say he or she feels is the reason for you talking? Text your teen right now and ask, *"Why do you think I talk to you?"*

By this point, with all the times I'm asking you to text your teens, they're probably thinking you're either having a nervous breakdown, dying, started drinking, or going through the change of life! With somewhat of a smirk on my face, I'm trying to show you that you have to be about asking and looking for an invitation to have discussions. You must listen to what they're thinking, rather than bully your way into communication by demanding they listen to what you have to say. You've had your turn the first twelve years of their life. Now it is their turn to talk and your turn to listen. I'm going to give you eight suggestions that I use to enhance discussion with the teens I spend time with.

1. Watch your parenting style! Here are three that are no longer effective in this teen culture.

Let me describe these styles in a different way.

I've never heard a mother say, "I want my daughter to be perfect."

I've never heard a dad say, "I'm going to rule my home with an iron fist."

And I've never heard any couple say, "We want to be judgmental parents."

However, I've heard hundreds of young ladies say, "My mom wants me to be perfect."

I've heard hundreds of young men say, "My dad rules with an iron fist...I can't wait to get away from home." And I've heard thousands of kids say, "My parents are the most judgmental people I know." Perfection, an authoritarian approach, and the conveyance of being judgmental are all approaches that just don't work. If you're saying, "Mark, now wait a minute!" Please don't hear, "Parents shouldn't want good, if not great, things for their kids." And please don't take my comments about an authoritarian approach to mean that parents don't have authority in their home. And never take my remarks about being judgmental as me stating that parents shouldn't be able to talk about their opinions or have their own observations about certain people and actions happening in the world. I'm not saying that.

What I am saying is that the culture has changed so much in recent years, that from a teen's perspective, the parent wants him or her to be perfect, pushing that child away. The culture teens live in (which is an appearance and performance world) is demanding they be perfect as well. If teens come home from a school that demands perfection (from their perspective) to a home that wants the same, they won't get any rest from this culture.

Furthermore, what I am saying about the authoritarian approach (the style my parents taught me) is that it is no longer effective, as kids don't have respect for those in authority. They should, but they don't. The cultural media bombardment, which is critical and never-ending, doesn't portray anyone in authority as one to be respected.

In addition, the judgmental demeanor that a teen sees only pushes them away, as the culture has become somewhat volatile towards anyone who might be critical, disapproving, or negative towards another.

The change has happened in the culture. So, if you want to be effective in connecting with our teens who are living in this culture, then, as wise parents, choose a different path of engaging, so you don't lose the relationship with your teen.

2. Quit correcting all the time.

Mom, Dad, give it a break. If all your children hear is your constant correction, then they will tune you out in a heartbeat and won't listen to any of the wisdom you have to offer. The tendency we all have as parents is to correct our kids, help them make adjustments, and improve what we see in their behavior and way of thinking. We all do that. Yet, with this cultural change, where all they hear (in this appearance and performance world) is that they'll never measure up, they've got to have a place to break from the constant demand for change. I see this play out all the time at our residential counseling center, where I live with sixty struggling high school kids from around the country. If all I did was correct their every mistake and told them how to be better and do things correctly, I would never have any time to build or further my relationship with them. I would become nothing more than a correctional officer, patrolling my household to ensure that no one did anything wrong.

I know this: Teens don't change because of correction or the display of authority; they change because of a relationship. And I hope that their key relationship is with you.

I'm sure of this: If you always correct your son, he'll never grow into a man, and when he ages out of your home, you won't see him too often. If you always correct your daughter, she'll find someone else to give her value, and you'll find her moving further and further away from correction to find a connection, but not with you.

3. Spend more time listening than talking.

If you can get them to put their phone down and you can pry yours out of your hands for a few minutes, spend some time asking questions and just listen. Whenever they respond, just listen without making comments, suggestions, or giving observations, unless your teens ask, "What do you think?" Those are the words you're hoping and longing for.

It sounds odd, but when you do take the time to listen to your teens, you create an atmosphere where they will invite you to "come into" a conversation. That doesn't mean that you don't have to be the one who stands at the door and knocks, but wait for the invitation.

Last year, our twelve-year-old granddaughter, Macie, was living with us, along with her whole family, as they were building a new home when their old home sold quickly. They lived with us for eight months—all four of them.

On one of the nights, Macie had a meltdown. She got upset, let everyone know it, and stormed up the stairs to her room and cried. A few yelling matches ensued, and I was quick to make sure that I didn't interfere with my daughter and son-in-law's parenting. So I asked their permission, "Can I talk to her?"

I walked upstairs, knocked on her door, and asked if I could come in. She said yes, rather reluctantly, so I went into the room and laid down on the bed with her. I said nothing for about ten minutes. She was crying, and once she calmed, I asked her, "Want to hear what I think?" She said, "No." My question was too soon, as emotion was still playing with her little heart, so I just lay there quietly. After another ten minutes, I asked, "I have a thought… want to know what it is?"

Her response? "Sure."

If she would have said no, I would have left it alone and told her "good night, I love you, and see you tomorrow." But she said, yes. So I wanted to make sure that I was speaking to her heart and listening to what she had to say. That was the important part—what she had to say, not what I wanted to say. Quite honestly, I can't even remember what the issue was, and I don't really remember what she talked about. But I do know this: She listened because I first listened to her.

Have you noticed how young people like to talk to older people? Have you ever noticed that the older men get, the bigger their ears get? Perhaps it's because, in God's divine plan, He wants us to listen more, speak less, be slow to anger, and quick to hear. I like to listen.

4. Determine your discussions to be over a long period of time, rather than just a quick conversation with a beginning and an end.

I mentioned this earlier. Very few major issues facing kids today can be resolved or directed in one conversation. Keep your discussions open-ended. State it like this, "Well, let's talk about that later after I've given it some thought." And don't hesitate to say, "You know, I don't know…let me think about that."

5. Ask questions, and toss the ball to them so they can "reflect" on another idea or thought that might stimulate them to think deeper.

I've asked you a bunch of questions in this series…all designed to get you to think, perhaps differently. I find that if I spend more time cultivating the land and stirring up what has already been planted, I can get more out of the conversation. So, I do that by asking questions to whatever answer they give me in a conversation.

Capiche?

6. Keep the discussion about them and only share your opinion when asked.

A fool finds no pleasure in understanding, but delights in airing their own opinions. (Proverbs 18:2)

Share your opinion when asked, and don't use the conversation as your platform for opinion distribution. Remember, the conversation should be about them and for them; this isn't about you.

7. Every conversation doesn't have to have a lesson.

This idea bears repeating.

I recently sat and listened to a mom have a conversation with her daughter, and I felt like she was reading from an outline. She meant well in wanting to make her seventeen-year-old daughter understand what she was talking about, but she treated her more like a ten-year-old. I lost respect for the way she talked to her daughter.

It was a *lesson* that began with point one and ended with point seven. It was almost as if she couldn't leave well enough alone. She had already made her point, but she felt the need to explain everything. I didn't know whether Mom was clueless to the age of her teen or just trying to find value by displaying how well thought-out her decision was by sharing the sequence of her logic.

Needless to say, her daughter shut her down when the first word came out of her mouth. Simply put, have a conversation, but don't hold a "class." Have a conversation without a lesson. Not every teachable moment has to have a lesson tagged onto it.

8.   Sometimes silence is the best response and greatest answer.

Even fools are thought to be wise if they keep silent, and discerning if they hold their tongues. (Proverbs 17:8)

Is this a common thread that people hear me say about parenting teens? Sure it is. Because when communicating with a teen, it is more important to listen to what is being said than making sure you, as a mom or dad, are saying the right things. Some of my best counseling sessions with kids have me saying the following wise words:

"Hmmmmmm"

"Really?"

"Wow!"

"Oh."

"You're kidding me…."

"Are you serious?"

"And then what happened?"

"I'm sorry."

"Wooooowwww...."

Usually, a kid gets up from a time where my words are nothing more than these and says, "Man, that was the best counseling session I've ever had." It's because I was more intent on listening than I was on talking. Put down the phone, and pick up the conversation that your kids are dying to have with you.

CHAPTER 14

Giving Your Teens What They Want

Tell your children about it in the years to come, and let your children tell their children. Pass the story down from generation to generation.

Joel 1:3 (NLT)

In case you haven't noticed, teens communicate differently today than we did when we were teens. The Internet ushered in a new way of not only communicating, but also finding information, answers to questions, instructions to live by, entertainment that never quits, and new ways of social networking. Teens may think they are making tons of friends on the World Wide Web. They may feel like they are communicating with the whole world. However, the reality is that talking, making friends, commenting, and meeting on the Internet isn't the same as talking face-to-face, sharing meals, getting together, and hanging out. These newly found Internet *relationships* many times lack real involvement and investment in one another's life.

Internet posts on just about any social network depict lives that are idyllic in appearance and performance. Conversation is more about the transfer of information. It's about a *daily diary* of what one is doing communicated through pictures and hashtags. It's mostly one-sided, a scream for attention, and self-satisfied when all the *likes* and pretty, superficial comments come rolling in.

I'm not saying all the impact of the Internet is bad. I believe the good from it far outweighs the negatives that are given much more attention. The way teens communicate begs for deeper interaction, and parents have the perfect opportunity to fill the communication and connection gap most teens feel.

To understand the need for your involvement in the lives of your kids, it's important to understand the world of communication and cultural influence they live in. You need to know what you're fighting against to make sure your intentional message of leaving a legacy isn't lost in the white noise surrounding your teens.

A Culture of Negativity

There's a benefit to filling out surveys, writing reviews, stating opinions, and reflecting on experiences. There's something to be said for critiquing services, rating the performance of a business, or sharing a perspective or opinion on just about anything. People want to be heard, and the Internet now provides a way to speak, regardless of whether or not anyone is listening. Quite honestly, I think it will remain part of our culture for years to come.

People want to be heard, and the Internet now provides a way to speak, regardless of whether or not anyone is listening.

The negative side effort of rating every business, every politician, and every service is we have become a world where too many consider themselves *judge and jury*.

Given time, anyone can find fault with anything. There will be a bad meal served at a restaurant that has served thousands of great meals. There will always be mistakes, shortcomings, disappointments, and unmet expectations as long as man is alive. If you look hard enough and deep enough into anybody's background, you can find faults, discover disappointments, learn about their mistakes, and obtain information that can be misused to trash them. The negativity of the culture has exploded. People are critical, complaining, yelping, rating everyone's performance, and sharing opinions publicly. Everyone now has the *right* to complain and the ability to put those complaints out there on the Internet for the world to see.

People do have the right to complain. But it doesn't mean they should. To me, constant complaining counters the first verses of Matthew 7, which states,

> *Judge not, that you be not judged. For with what judgment you judge, you will be judged; and with the measure you use, it will be measured back to you. And why do you look at the speck in your brother's eye, but do not consider the plank in your own eye?* (Matthew 7:1-3, NKJV)

Today, we live in a culture that considers negativity just *being real.* The problem with negativity being the norm lies in the fact that it creates an absence of positive messages to counterbalance the constant stream of bad stuff. In other words, so much time is spent focusing on and explaining the negative, that little time is spent clarifying and illuminating anything positive. Teens don't hear positive anymore. They hear where they failed, didn't measure up, and what they need to do better next time.

An Atmosphere of Know-It-Alls

Secondly, this culture of negativity is filled with know-it-alls and self-proclaimed authorities who really believe they've cornered and mastered certain roles because they've tried or experienced something once or twice. Sharing personal experiences becomes a platform interpreted as wise and authoritative merely because it is videoed, blogged about, or printed.

I don't write this book based on what I learned from being a parent or grandparent. I am a parent of two and a grandparent of four, but that hardly makes me an expert when it comes to helping folks connect with their kids. What gives me the platform to speak on parenting is my work with thousands of families. I have seen firsthand the significant impact, and ways parents and grandparents are indeed creating a legacy of influence for their teens.

I recently watched a video of a young lady who has an autistic son. She shared the ways she thought everyone should handle their autistic children. I've seen plenty of videos and blogs of new fathers sharing what they are learning about fatherhood. They have infants, and they are already online telling everyone else how they should parent. Suddenly, these new dads are the experts. I've seen and listened to many who adopted one child. Now they evidently know how to counsel everyone else on how to raise an adopted child. It's like everyone has suddenly become an expert because they have a platform where they can share. A blog is practically viewed as a doctoral degree, allowing just about anyone to think he is a specialist because of one experience.

That's about as sensible as calling me a veterinarian because I helped a vet sew up one of our horses who had a deep cut, or call me an obstetrician because I delivered my own son. Maybe I'm a preacher because I spoke from a pulpit. I'm not a dentist just because I brushed my teeth this morning.

Sharing one's perspective does not make one a professional. Her own personal story alone does not give the writer or blogger the credentials to lead others. As parents, we know this because we've been around the block a few times and understand that just because you see something or read something doesn't mean it's automatically the truth. It does not mean it is totally accurate either. It's just one person's perspective based on what they saw or felt.

Teens are falling hook, line, and sinker for many people's foolishness because they know no better. They interpret information as wisdom. They can hardly tell the difference between the two. Two things happen when everyone is a know-it-all or a so-called expert. One, it creates a world of false wisdom. Two, it inflates many people to believe they know more than they really do. Hey, I can change spark plugs in my car, but I'm not a mechanic.

A World of Fantasy

Third, a world of fantasy existence combined with geographical contentment has captured many teens. In plain English, that means many teens and even young adults are happy to stay holed up in their bedrooms posting their observations, hopes, and a whole lot of selfies on social media rather than going out and engaging with the real world. They remain where they are instead of moving forward to a better situation in life. Change takes self-discipline and drive, and they don't have any to help them improve, grow, or mature. They use social media posts and affirmations as validation that they are doing great, when in reality, they may not be.

Here's an example. I recently saw a post on Facebook where a young lady stated she finally feels content with her life. She found a new confidence to face everything before her. She stated she used to be goofy with her words, crazy in her actions, and immature in the way she related to people. She added that she used to view her appearance negatively, but now is satisfied and pleased with where she is.

I was excited for this young lady that she developed newfound confidence in herself. Then I read

Kids use social media posts and affirmations as validation that they are doing great, when in reality, they may not be.

the comments of all her *friends*, and they alarmed me. All one hundred ten of them affirmed everything this young lady said she was feeling. That sounds great on the surface, but the truth is, the young lady still struggles with many of the issues she now thinks she *used to* have. In their desire to stay on trend, the friends' comments completely skipped over the truth. Now I don't think Facebook is the right forum to *speak the truth in love*, but if this young lady takes these comments to the bank, she may not take steps to progress in the ways that will help her succeed in real-life situations.

Truthfully, this lady is a wonderful young lady, however, she is obnoxious. She is goofy to be around. She acts crazy at times. She's very immature for her age. If she doesn't work to make some changes physically, she'll likely face serious health problems in the future. The oh-so-encouraging comments addressed none of these issues. Again, I am glad no one called her out on social media, but if she counts on social media as her only belief system, will she accept truth from anywhere else if it's hard to hear?

There needs to be someone in this young lady's life who speaks the truth so she can become better, reach her potential for deep relationships, find significance, and go places to use her gifts and talents. Contentment quickly changes to complacency, and motivation to move to a better place gets lost.

It's not the presence of the negative but the absence of the positive that causes a problem.

I said earlier it's not the presence of the negative but the absence of the positive that causes a problem. Let me add that inundating youth with shallow positivity and no healthy motivation also damages. Hearing only positive comments to the point of pretending nothing negative exists, sometimes hurts more than it helps.

This new culture is difficult for teens to navigate. On the one hand, the cultural tone (political, doom-and-gloom attitudes about the climate, gender wars, left vs. right, and more) is so negative it has teens worried, walking on pins and needles about their future. False information from so-called experts leads them to second guess what they hear and read. People commit horrific acts like rape and murder and broadcast them live on social media. On the other hand, teens' social media circles go overboard in their praise of what is sometimes patently ridiculous.

It's like that old children's fable of the emperor and his new clothes.

142

At the end of the story, the emperor marches through the streets naked, foolishly convinced he is wearing fine garments. Even more foolishly, his subjects all pretend he is fully clothed too. They praise the beautiful new outfit the emperor wears, and he is stark naked as a jaybird.

Even though teens want to believe it, fake affirmation causes them not to trust what they hear, wondering whether they are really being told the truth.

This cultural struggle provides a perfect setting for parents to enter. In a world of negative, know-it-alls, and half-truths, your teen is looking for a positive, trustworthy speaker of the truth in love. Your voice of tried-and-true experience can rise above the white noise that drowns out sensible and wise advice. That's your call. Will you accept it?

You can be a voice in the darkness of this world that gently offers what your kids are desperately searching for. Speak truth, whether they seem like they are listening or not. When they hear something completely different from those around them, but they're not quite sure who to believe, your history with them of love and support can convince them you're the one who's telling it straight.

Giving Your Teens What They Want
(Even When They Don't Know They Want It)

Recently, when I was traveling, I stopped at a well-known burger joint inside the airport. I ordered a cheeseburger (medium rare, no onions) and fries. With anticipation, I awaited what I understood would be the best burger ever. However, when the waitress brought my order to the table, the hamburger was burned to a crisp, there were onions everywhere, and they brought onion rings instead of fries. I didn't get what I wanted.

I told the waitress, and she said they'd fix it. Fifteen minutes later, they brought out a medium-rare hamburger with no cheese. There were fries this time, but I still wanted a medium-rare cheeseburger. I told the waitress I ordered a cheeseburger, and I still didn't get one. She apologized, took the plate back, and vowed to get it right this time. Third time is the charm, right? Not in this case. The third time around, I got a medium-rare cheeseburger with fries. The only problem was the onions on the burger. I still didn't get what I wanted or ordered.

I said thanks, promptly took all my belongings and left. I had no time to get another meal elsewhere. My flight was about to depart. I didn't get what I wanted. I felt frustrated. I was still hungry as I got on the plane. At that point, I wanted to eat anything. I had to settle for airline snacks because the place I had anticipated disappointed me greatly.

I expected something satisfying. When it disappointed me, and I didn't get it, my hunger pangs drove me to settle for something far less than what I really longed for. My hunger got satisfied but not with what I wanted. Now every time I see that burger joint, I remember the failed cheeseburger experience, and I turn away. My sense of disappointment remains, not only in the burger place but also in a waitress who really had no interest in taking care of my order or me.

This scenario reminds me of the Scripture from Luke 11:11-12 that says,

> *Which of you fathers, if your son asks for a fish, will give him a snake instead? Or if he asks for an egg, will give him a scorpion?*

In this scenario, if the son doesn't get what he wants, eventually he'll leave and go elsewhere so his hunger can be satisfied. Parents can give kids a satisfying meal of wisdom when their culture and social circles offer them an *incorrect order* of foolishness. Teens are asking for *fish* and *egg* to fuel their lives. Often they're given only cotton candy, the *fluff* of information overload, instead.

Teens don't come to parents to get more information. They usually come to ask questions. They are seeking insight and direction. This offers the perfect opportunity for you to share your mistakes, failures, and struggles.

After all, they are the source of much of your wisdom.

Quite honestly, information is a dime a dozen. It can be found anywhere and shared by anyone. Google, Siri, or Alexa can provide facts and details. That kind of stuff is not what your children are looking or hoping for. Again, they are looking for wisdom, the ability to use experience and knowledge to make good decisions and judgments. Information is communicated in the teaching model; wisdom is shared in the training model.

Information is communicated in the teaching model; wisdom is shared in the training model.

One of my greatest concerns for teens today is how many are viewing Scripture as information, not wisdom. Because they're in an information world, they categorize Scripture as just another historical reference, a good story, more material to process, or a mere set of data that is part of their family tradition.

What they want to know is how Scripture relates to them. How can the Bible help them get to a great place in life? That's the wisdom from the Scriptures, but it needs to be presented in a way that seems applicable to their real lives. Parents can share that.

For example, Scripture clearly states that sex within marriage is the only form of sexual relations of which God approves (Hebrews 13:4, 1 Thessalonians 4:3, Jude 7, Colossians 3:5, Galatians 5:19, 1 Corinthians 5:1, 2 Corinthians 12:21). For many teens, this is just information from a dusty document. How does it work today? Why would it make sense to swim against a very sexualized culture, when sex is fun? Why should teens deny themselves when everyone else is doing (and flaunting) it?

Here's where they need wisdom—the wisdom you have and can give. This wisdom is more than repeating the Scriptures they already know. This wisdom explains why this principle should be followed. It gives practical examples of the benefits and drawbacks of following the culture or following the Bible. A parent might communicate the wisdom packed in these verses in the following way:

> In all my years, I've heard and lived by the same principles my parents taught me. This is what I found. Sex before marriage has an unbelievable way of causing confusion in relationships. So, if this is the girl you're going to one day marry, make sure you work hard not to confuse the relationship. Work hard not to 'muddy the waters' with the one you will spend the rest of your life with.

This sample conversation includes not only the truth and information they've been given, but it lets them hear the importance of this principle. It emphasizes how it is relevant to them. In a world of information bombardment, can you dig deep and give them wisdom? When they ask for what they want, give it to them in a way that equips them to counter what the culture offers. Help them leave your table of conversation satisfied, not hungry, so they won't accept phony substitutes or shallow facts to satisfy their longings.

This wisdom is usually shared through stories of failures, successes, and lessons learned. These transform information into a true-to-life experience that can affect their choices and selections in life. Share your wisdom with intentionality. Don't just blow smoke in their ears, and don't tell the stories of your life for the satisfaction of telling them. (Remember the old folks who detailed their health ailments and scared their grandchildren and me away?) Tell them to offer a balance in their unbalanced world. Tell them to speak the truth in love, with affirmations of good and encouragement to mature in areas of much-needed growth.

The Art of Storytelling

Most times, wisdom and hope are shared through stories that include a concept or nugget of truth that sticks in your children's minds because the stories give them something they want.

Do you tell good stories? Can you think of the funniest moments in your life? How about the most bittersweet? What did you learn from the best and worst times of your life? What memories bring a smile to your face? What tales could grab the attention of your children as you sit around the dinner table or in front of a fireplace talking? Your life stories help your children get to know you better, but they can also help them examine their own lives in light of the choices you've made.

Surely you have plenty of stories you can weave into *morality tales*. A morality tale is a story with a lesson of right and wrong. Make sure each of your stories have a punch line of truth, something that they will remember. Don't overdo it. Often, just one line is enough. Make them think and leave them wanting more.

Making kids laugh is wonderful. It's a true gift when you can attach a life truth that you've gathered and now want to pass along. Earlier, I mentioned a comment made to me that changed my life. A dear fellow named Dave Tillack told a story. Then he said the infamous line (for me it was anyway) that stuck with me.

"When you're called to be a servant, don't stoop to be a king," Dave said.

I don't remember the story, but I will forever remember that one line.

Some of the most impactful stories I tell teens are the ones where I share my own humanity. I admit my mistakes and struggles. I reveal my vulnerability. I've learned to pull the humor out of all those stories, and I aim to keep it to one point per story. Ten lessons in one tale would make the tale not very interesting (more like a lecture) or too hard to take in and apply. (Why waste all those great things teens need to be taught?)

Practice your stories, even out loud in front of the mirror. Think about the funniest comedians. They take real-life situations and bring out the extraordinary. They admit when they acted foolishly or saw other people do something silly. They practice these routines again and again. Then they perform them over and over, honing and perfecting their craft. The best comics leave us wanting more by bringing their humorous anecdotes back around to something more serious. They leave us with a heartfelt lesson they've learned. We love their routines because we can relate.

Think back over your life. Jot down some stories or say them into a voice recorder. Play them back and listen to yourself. Are they funny? Do they come across as judgmental? Do they have a subtle message? Try your stories on your spouse first. Gauge his or her response and weigh the input carefully. You can leave a legacy of life lessons shared in the most entertaining ways. That's what I try to do with my own grandkids. I want my grandkids to say, "Remember when Poppa told us about…?" Or, "Hey, Poppa, tell us the story about…"

> I find most truths transfer best through stories, ones that are unique in origin and simple in approach.

I find most truths transfer best through stories, ones that are unique in origin and simple in approach. A story is easy to remember. Share yours. Include a point, but don't give it away too easily. Let them figure out how it applies to their own lives.

Every parent has stories. The ones that make a difference offer a point or purpose, packed inside a good dose of humor and transparent vulnerability.

The Intentionality of Sharing Wisdom

I'm convinced sharing wisdom doesn't always come naturally and doesn't transfer just by *hanging out*. Parents must choose to be intentional in order to impart something special that brings wisdom to the lives of their kids.

I was on the phone last night with a man who said he was going to hang out with his granddaughter over the weekend. He planned to spend some time with her as this twelve-year-old struggled to handle her parents' divorce. Her school performance slipped, appetite fled, interest in her extracurricular activities waned, and she isolated herself. She wanted to quit the activities she loved.

Her granddad wanted to help her get through this tragic time in her life by hanging out, but this young lady needed some guidance and direction. That takes more than just hanging out. I'm sure she longed to talk about her feelings, learn how to verbalize her frustrations, and know that it's okay to have a hard time dealing with this major loss in her life. Her actions (or inactivity) and attitudes clearly showed she was asking for help and a little bit of hope. This well-meaning grandpa planned to offer a time of activities and entertainment, but trying to cheer his granddaughter up or distract her from her problems wasn't going to fix the big issue in her life or help her process anything.

I encouraged the granddad to spend some time having fun, but also to plan a time to sit down and open the door to share some wisdom. Maybe it could take place at an ice cream stand, a coffee shop, or her favorite pizza place. But he needed to create an atmosphere of connection more than just fun and activity.

When you have moments to sit down and enjoy each other's company, but a larger issue like divorce still needs to be addressed, I would say something like the following.

Sweetheart, I know it's tough when a family is going through a divorce. I know it's a little complicated and you have so many feelings inside your head and heart. I want you to know if you ever need to talk to someone who has big ears and can listen well, I'm here for you. We can have fun, as I always do with you, but I want you to know I'm not afraid to talk about the tough stuff that you're going through too. Understand what I'm saying?

She may not say anything other than, *uh-huh.* But at the very least, in this situation, the granddaughter knows her grandparent is available to listen and offer hope in a situation she considers hopeless.

Over time, teens come back and share with parents (or grandparents) who invite them to do so. If you don't offer anything more than a good time, teens might believe you only want to keep things light and can't deal with the harder things in life. Or they might feel you love them when all is going well, but you can't (and won't) handle them when anything is wrong. Walk the tightrope of conversational wisdom with your teen. If you fall, get back up and try again. Be intentional about sharing the wisdom you possess that can help them.

Exposing the Truth in Love

Teens need to hear the truth in a way that does not feel judgmental or cloaked as a demand for perfection. It's a delicate dance. Parents need to learn not to gloss over what is going on in their kids' lives with total praise and good times together, but also to tread lightly at first when introducing heavy subjects. Give them the opportunity to come to you anytime, and don't push or prod too hard. When you strike the right balance, kids feel comfortable having deeper discussions.

Here's a word for any grandparent who may also be reading this book. Grandparents need to land right in the middle, not an authoritarian who points out every imperfection and not the loving people who see everything their grandchildren do as sunshine and roses. If you see your grandchildren quite a bit, then it would be wrong not to mention concerns you have. I want my grandkids to know I'm going to love them to pieces, but I will speak into whatever issue comes up. I'm going to speak about the elephant in the room. Confront the obvious. Push past the discomfort of bringing up what we may never have talked about before. But that can't be my main purpose in being a grandparent. Our roles as grandparents are much more than correction.

When you do speak to an issue, make sure you do so in a spirit of love. Don't talk about sore subjects when you are angry. Most likely they'll still be there once you cool off. Approach tough subjects with the intent to help. You are not in their lives to prove to yourself or anyone else that your way of handling their messes and mistakes is the only right way. You are there to support, encourage, complement parents in correction, and communicate calm wisdom.

Here are some things you can cross off your list. Phrases like these will only offend and push your children away:

- You look like you're gaining weight.
- Why can't you do things like your brother/sister?
- I told you so.
- If you only used your head
- Well, your actions aren't telling me anything different!
- You always do this! Or, You never do that!
- I don't think you can do it.
- Did you wash your hair this morning?
- Why don't you have better friends?

All of these are veiled judgments in the form of questions. They may hold truth, but they do not communicate love and acceptance. You can try to retract hurtful statements immediately, but they won't be forgotten. Kids internalize harsh statements immediately. Your apology may be accepted, but the sting remains. If you ever have to explain what you mean, then you

Shame-based comments push teens further into inappropriate behavior they are exhibiting to cover the inadequacy they feel.

should have done your homework and practiced a bit before allowing words of shame to come out of your mouth or in your writings to them.

Shame-based comments push teens further into inappropriate behavior they are exhibiting to cover the inadequacy they feel. A well-spoken word counters insecurity, inadequacy, and negativity. It gives values to the one who hears it. Positive words say, "You matter." Choose your words carefully. When words damage and harm, the one who said them quickly gets put on the list of teens' favorite people to avoid.

Here's what one young man shared about his grandfather. Which category did he put his Grandpa in?

> Grandpa always listened to me first. Then he would share a story that made his perspective interesting. He had an unbelievable way of being positive when he was sharing something negative about me. He looked me straight in the eye, and I knew I was loved, listened to, and corrected in a way that made me always want to come back for more.

(I share a couple of stories in this chapter about grandparents because they sometimes possess wisdom about communication that I wish I had as a parent. While some grandparents are lousy at communication, many possess a timeliness about when to enter the conversation that might just be a good lesson to learn.)

Wow! That is high praise from a teen. Believe me. Don't you want your children to describe you in those terms? If so, speak to their issues with a great sense of love. Be intentional about taking advantage of the time you have to share wisdom. Pull them out of their fantasy worlds of social media and into real life. Practice your stories and tell them with laughter and a great message.

You can be the one who counters the culture of negativity. You can be parents who bring balance to the off-kilter world your kids live in. That's giving your children what they really want.

Since Nagging and Lecturing Don't Work, Try Something Different!

My dear brothers and sisters, take note of this: Everyone should be quick to listen, slow to speak and slow to become angry.

James 1:19

I think you know by now I tend to tell it like it is. So I'm warning you up front. This chapter may step on some parents' toes. As the kids say today, "Sorry, not sorry." It's important to talk about certain communication styles many parents employ. I'm focusing on two styles in particular—nagging and lecturing. Stop. Just stop it. They don't work. Leave the nagging and lecturing in your children's early years. If you keep these bad communication habits when your kids become teens, I predict you will destroy your relationships.

Okay, I'm going to make some assumptions here. In most families, mothers do more of the nagging, while fathers have a propensity to lecture. Let me set the background for my theories. Moms love teaching their kids. Watching little ones grow, develop, and begin verbal engagement is absolutely wonderful. Moms get in the habit of teaching. Kids through the age of twelve need to be taught. It's the right model. Teaching involves repetition, constant questions, continuous urging, and helping with appearance and behavior. Moms do a wonderful job at this. They desire the very best in the lives of their little children. I venture to say moms get more involved in the lives of their kids during the first twelve years than dads do. Am I getting myself in trouble here?

Dads love to transfer thoughts, opinions, and the lessons they've learned to their kids. But when children are young, dads pretty much

If you keep these bad communication habits when your kids become teens, I predict you will destroy your relationships.

stay in *let's play* mode. When those little kids turn twelve or thirteen, dads spring into action. Suddenly, their kids need to take more responsibility, start growing up, learn some lessons, and hear about the duties in life. Many dads

believe they will miss their window of opportunity if they don't gather their messages together and start lecturing. Their lectures are meant well, but lectures are talks or speeches given to teach. They work well with groups (of adults, mostly). They can be disasters when focused on an audience of one. A lecture is for teaching, not training. A discussion is by far the better route, where the focus of the conversation is not on what Dad has to share, but more on what a child wants to learn.

One daughter I know described her dad as a know-it-all who never wanted to listen to anyone. "He might as well go into a room, look into the mirror, and have a conversation with himself. He needs no one else to talk to," she said. That should not be a dad's reputation with his kids. Of course, I'm sure moms lecture at times, just as there are times dads nag. Both can take note here.

A Google search of the *Oxford Dictionaries* for the definition of the verb *nag* defines it as: "to annoy or irritate [a person] with persistent fault-finding or continuous urging." The *Merriam-Webster Dictionary* defines *nagging* as: "to annoy [someone] by often complaining about his or her behavior, appearance, etc.; to annoy [someone] with repeated questions, requests, or orders; to cause [someone] to feel annoyed or worried for a long period of time."

Most parents tend to communicate through repetition, which is needed before adolescence, but it must be transitioned away from when kids hit their teen years. What was once an effort to help them through multiple reminders, now irritates. In a sentence, some parents *tell you what they're going to tell you, then they tell you, then they tell you what they just told you.* And if that doesn't work to get someone's attention or change their behavior or thoughts, then they'll say it again. I'm exaggerating a little, but you get my point.

> *A nagging wife* [or parent] *is like the dripping of a leaky roof in a rainstorm. Stopping her is like trying to stop the wind. It's like trying to grab olive oil with your hand.* (Proverbs 27:15-16, NIRV)

The nag annoys with repeated requests or orders that might sound like these:

- Did you remember what I told you?
- Did you remember today is so-and-so's birthday?
- Did you clean up after yourself?
- Do I need to repeat myself?
- Are you listening to me?
- Did you buy a Christmas gift for your brother?
- Did you take care of…?
- Why isn't that done yet?

The nag never stops. They wonder why they get responses like these:

- Okay, okay, I get it.
- Stop! I understood you the first time.
- I heard you the first time!
- No, I didn't hear you. I just wanted to hear you repeat it again. (Insert sarcasm here.)
- You don't need to tell me again!
- I'll get on it when I have time!
- I'm not an idiot!

You should recognize that these responses are all spoken out of frustration. If they don't snap back at you, your child may instead shut down and shut you out. This is how teens think when someone continually reminds them of what to do, what to remember, or how to behave. Your daughter thinks you believe her to be incompetent and irresponsible. Your son thinks you're telling him he can't be trusted to complete a project. Your children will get the message that you think they are inadequate, immature, and ignorant. Are you trying to communicate that they're not capable of handling what's in front of them? Well, that's the message you send when you nag. That's what they hear.

And you know what? Your kids might be incompetent, irresponsible, untrustworthy, inadequate, and ignorant. They're still learning. They're still kids. But bigger kids want and need to do more figuring out on their own. Sometimes they fail. Sometimes they don't handle the requests put before them very well.

Nagging eliminates influence. Nagging at teens also inspires rebellion. It makes teens vow not to do whatever it is you are nagging about, just to spite you. The more you nag, the less they listen. If nagging becomes the norm, they will eventually write you off. Teens who feel inadequate when nagged will try to get away from those hurtful experiences by cutting you out of all future conversations. You'll miss out on your call to connect with your children, and they'll miss out on all your wisdom because they've turned you off.

One young man described his mom as one who always felt the need to focus on the negative. She demeaned her kids. She may have wanted to do a good thing by pointing out areas where her kids could improve. But her presentation came out all wrong. Her family expected her indictments of them whenever they saw her coming, so they eventually just wrote her off. Sadly, this young

Nagging at teens eliminates influence and also inspires rebellion.

man reported his mother was such a nag and so negative that no one missed her when she passed.

Teens need parents to focus on them, but not only on the parts of them that need improvement. Put your emphasis on the interests of your children. Extend grace, not condemnation. Nagging focuses on what they aren't doing. Instead, focus on the good things they are doing. I think I've nagged about this nagging enough.

If you recognize yourself in any part of this chapter, you have time to change. You're still breathing, so you still have time to try a different approach with your children. I hope you'll take my words as an encouragement to shift your style of parenting from what was effective in your kids' early years to a more effective and much-needed positive training model that offers the best of you to the not-so-great in them.

Truth be told, your kids probably hate your lectures. They love your stories, but they can't stand your lectures. Lectures are ineffective and bore your kids to death. Conversations and discussions are two-way streets. No one's eyes should glaze over. Aim for dialogues, not monologues, with your children.

Remember to unpack your wisdom over time and in many conversations. Some topics may come up for years. Some may be addressed only once. You don't have to *play the whole deck* in one talk as if you will never have your child's attention again. If one of you were on your deathbed, then I would understand this technique. If not, go easy. I know you want to transfer your sage advice so your children's world will get better and they won't suffer the consequences as you did. That's a great goal, but it needs to be met over time. Make sure you move from lectures to discussions.

Lecture works well during the teaching phase of your children's lives. Discussion works better and is much more suited to their adolescent years. Lecturing puts the focus on you, taking attention away from your kids. Teens want someone to listen, not just talk at them.

Teens tune out lectures with the rolling of the eyes, a glance at others in the room (clearly communicating, *here we go again*), or by mentioning other commitments they suddenly need to honor. Lecture works well in the classroom. When your teen children are with you, they're not in a classroom. They're in your presence, where training should take place with them. The Christian life is more *caught* than *taught*.

Try Something Different

Be brief. I prefer half-dozen ten-minute discussions to an hour-long one. While I wish we could sit down for hours and talk, most teens aren't accustomed to sitting still and being attentive that long. Most have not been trained to be able to do so. When teens walk away from me, I want them to know I was interested in what they had to say, kept the conversation brief so they'd want to talk again, and believe we can think differently and still have great connecting conversations.

Take advantage of the times they approach you. My granddaughter recently came to me and asked if she could work for me. She wanted to make some gas money for transportation. My response was, "Sure. Come talk to me and tell me what you want." When she came over, I just said, "Hey, let's talk about your need for a job."

As we sat down, I asked a different question. "Do you think you'll drink alcohol when you're in college?" I asked. I asked the question casually, and she responded easily. We talked for a bit, and I was able to let her know how much I appreciate her opinions. I didn't share mine.

After ten minutes of talk, I transitioned the discussion to what she really came over for.

Take advantage of the times your teens come to you and want something. Turn them into opportunities to have one of those short discussions that help you get to know them and the beliefs and values they embrace as their own. I learned years ago I'm not afraid to briefly discuss heavier topics when they want something from me. It may seem like a bit of a conversational manipulation on my part, but it is worth it for the sake of a deeper connection.

Here's a fun way to get interesting conversations going. Have an All-Text Thursday (or any day) Dinner. What in the world is that? It goes like this. Set up a group text with everyone at the table for dinner. Let everyone know via group text that all conversation (I mean every word) will be communicated through texting. No talking. Not a peep out of anyone.

Text everyone when it's time to eat dinner. As all come to the table, have a prayer already written to be texted to everyone. Send the prayer. Then text "Amen." As you hear the notification *dings* around the table, start texting for someone to pass the potatoes. Next, text for someone to pass the meat. Then text for the vegetables. Have fun texting as the only form of communication for the night. Text if someone can get more tea or water for the meal. Text if someone can bring in dessert. Text and ask if all are enjoying the meal.

Then text the following question, "Hey, what's one thing you'd like to see different in your life?" Remember, you'll get a wide array of responses depending on the age of your children. But it's a different way to pry open the doors of their hearts and minds. Kids respond frankly via text. They say things they wouldn't say face-to-face. So this may be a way to get them to let their guard down and let you in more. You may be surprised at their answers. Use every creative means and opportunity to find out what they're thinking. Whatever they say, don't give your opinion. Just listen (or at All-Text Dinners, just read). Remember, no talking.

Over time, after a couple of All-Text Thursdays, ask a question that dives a little deeper into their hearts. Ask them, "Have you ever been depressed?" or "Do you know anyone who has thought about suicide?" or "What has been the hardest time of your life?"

You can always follow up and tell them that you'd love to talk about their answers, if they want. Don't nag. Don't lecture. Listen to their hearts. In time, they'll begin to ask you questions. Then you'll have your opportunity to give input into their lives.

Instead of Open-Ended Questions, Have Open-Ended Discussions

When I meet people on an airplane, I find sometimes it's easier to talk to strangers than people I've known for years. Interesting, eh? Maybe it's because all things are new. It's interesting to find out about their lives, and

Answer their questions with a touch of wisdom and leave room to have more and more discussions in the future.

I'm all ears to hear their stories. Perhaps trying this technique with your children would let them know that you are all ears about them. Sit down next to a child sometime. Extend your hand for a shake and introduce yourself. Say something like, "Hi, what's your name?" Act like you don't know where they're from, where they go to school, or anything about them. See what they have to share.

Hey, kids love to talk about themselves. Give them the opportunity. Eventually, they'll circle back and show more interest in you because you showed interest in them.

Keep asking questions and just wait for it. Wait for that magical moment when they ask that first question of importance. They'll eventually start asking you more questions that will lead to the discussions you long to have.

Picture it like this: You're on one side of the door of your children's hearts. They're on the other. Your words push on the door trying to open it. If you nag, the door won't budge. If you insist on making the relationship go your way, it's like pushing the door into their faces. Ouch!

With loving words over time, you find out you weren't supposed to be pushing on the door at all. You should have been pulling, gently tugging the handle with encouragement, love, and words of their value and worth. Soon, you'll find you have to back up because they're swinging the door wide open themselves to let you in.

So when they come around and ask you questions, don't give answers that bring you to a standstill. If you know you won't agree, stop the conversation while it's still pleasant. Answer their questions with a touch of wisdom and leave room to have more and more discussions in the future. If you don't have a good answer to their questions or you're not ready to share one, end your discussion with any of these comments to keep the conversation open-ended and ongoing. You can pick it up the next day or the next time you're able to talk together.

- I need to think about that before I answer.
- You know, I'm not sure, but I'll find out and circle back with you.
- I don't know. Can I get back with you?
- Wow, that's a tough one. I'm not sure. What do you think?
- Hey, I'm interested in your comments about this. Can we come back to it later?
- Man, that's a great question. I need some time to come up with a good answer.

A string of conversations that happen over a period of time has much more impact than one big conversation that tries to answer it all. Believe me, parents, it's not about the answer you give, but the way you engage that matters the most. Engage in the right ways, and as your children get older, you'll be the ones they come to for answers to the deeper questions of life.

Remind Once and Leave it Alone

This anti-repetition thing bears repeating. If they don't get it the first time you mention something to them, forget it. Don't harp, nag, or lecture. Move on, and let them suffer the consequence. Quit trying to rescue them from any possibility of failure. If it's their responsibility to remember or complete something, let them either remember it or forget it and pay the price. The consequences of forgetfulness or irresponsibility speak louder than your shaming words when they forget. You really only have to say it once. They'll listen better next time, or the time after that, or the time after that. (It takes longer for some than others. That's okay. Button it. Literally bite your tongue if you have to.)

Saying the same thing over and over expecting a different result is the definition of insanity, isn't it? Waiting for that magical light to pop on where she/he finally get it is treating your teen like a little child. Repetition makes your teens feel childish, immature, incapable and incompetent, not exactly the message that you want to convey to them.

Asking a question like, "Do you know that it's your dad's birthday next week?" may be meant as a gentle reminder. However, it can come across as insinuating they are too clueless to remember. Instead, ask a question in a way that shifts the focus to yourself. "I don't know what to get for your dad's birthday next week. What are you getting him?" Put the emphasis on yourself. That way, they don't feel like you think they're ignorant and can't remember it is someone special's birthday next week.

Quit Interrupting

The greatest barrier to effective conversation is interrupting. It's just rude. It comes across as arrogance. The second the interruption happens, a message is sent to your child that clearly states your thoughts are much more important than what he has to say. If you interrupt your children on a regular basis to insert your words of wisdom, soon they'll stop talking to you at all. Interruption pushes children far away from your presence. Interrupting obstructs engaging. There are a couple of Scriptures to guide you, verses that share the wisdom in listening first before answering.

The greatest barrier to effective conversation is interrupting. It's just rude.

Everyone should be quick to listen, slow to speak and slow to become angry. (James 1:19)

Let people finish speaking before you try to answer them. That way you will not embarrass yourself and look foolish. (Proverbs 18:13, ERV)

So let them speak. Sure, they'll stumble over words, repeat themselves, and say stupid things. Nine times out of ten you can guess what their next words will be. You might even feel bored. Still, you need to pay attention. Focus on listening to what they're truly searching for behind what they're trying to ask. They will soon learn that Mom and Dad understand them. More and more, your conversations will flourish because they know the discussions will be on their terms, about their agendas, not yours. Above all, you want your children to feel honored and respected because you give them your full attention when you listen.

Listen, discuss, and repeat. That's a model that builds close relationships and a lifetime of trust.

CHAPTER 16

Not Every Argument Needs to be Argued

Even fools are thought wise if they keep silent, and discerning if they hold their tongues.

Proverbs 17:28

It's everywhere! Turn on any news channel and you hear arguing. There are TV programs where the focus of interaction is to do nothing but argue. Newscasters love a good argument because it creates good stories. Teens argue back and forth on social sites. Adults argue their points of view in postings and blogs. Politicians spend their lives arguing for this or against that, and groups of people argue for their rights and their longing to be heard.

Teens fight to feel valued. *Will someone please listen to me?*

Young adults in their twenties and thirties fight to feel validated. *Will someone please listen to me?*

Older folks fight to be heard. *Will someone please listen to me?*

Notice a common thread in these? Everyone longs to be listened to. People master the art of arguing in hopes of being heard. That longing is born from a craving to be valued, a yearning to be appreciated and treasured and cherished. I would argue the underlying thread is the desire to be truly known. It is how we've been created to connect in relationships. It's hard to connect when no one listens.

Arguing flourishes today because people aren't listening to one another. When the art of listening disappears, people choose to quarrel, disagree, squabble, bicker, fight, wrangle, dispute, and feud. It's been that way since the beginning of time. The difference today is we have more tools and electronic gadgets to use to argue. Technology makes arguments more readily available and the capacity for not listening a little easier.

One group sees things one way, and another sees it a different way. There is something inherent in us to want other people to agree with us. We feel valued when we are in accord with each other. In the same way, we feel less valued when others do not agree with us.

The fight to express diverging or opposite views, usually in a heated exchange, is self-focused. If we are intent on persuading others to share our views at all costs, we are self-centered. It's a one-way street—our way or the highway. When two or more people engage in conversation in this manner, it's nothing but a fight. Consensus can't be gained because no one is entertaining anyone else's views. It's all *me first* thinking, with a goal of the meeting of personal needs rather than the needs of anyone else in the conversation. How does that kind of talk line up with this Scripture?

> *Don't have anything to do with foolish and stupid* arguments, *because you know they produce quarrels. And the Lord's servant must not be quarrelsome but must be kind to everyone, able to teach, not resentful.* (2 Timothy 2:23-24, emphasis added)

Some arguments sound good but are steeped in issues that violate everything you believe and hold to be true. Even so, the people making those arguments deserve to be heard. Why? Because all people need to feel valued, known, and heard or they won't be able to trust and listen to any other view. It may take everything you've got not to hotly defend biblically-based beliefs you hold dear, especially when you feel attacked. However, here's where your gentle answer can turn away anger. Your reasoned responses, delivered in ways that honor and respect the other person, allow them to hear a different belief without going on the defense.

The fight to express diverging or opposite views, usually in a heated exchange, is self-focused.

In a culture where arguments are the norm and resolution is rarely achieved, I suggest arguing isn't the best way to influence. Matter of fact, arguing with teens many times just solidifies their position and justifies their viewpoint.

Remember this: Not every argument needs to be argued.

I was with a fellow a few months ago who has been receiving quite a bit of criticism about his views on homosexuality. Adamantly opposed to the homosexual lifestyle, he has been bashed and bruised by some media outlets. Others applauded him for his stance and willingness to *speak the truth* and be a *voice in the wilderness*. He told me stories of what people are saying about him, revealed threats that have been thrown his way, and showed me how vicious people's responses have been to him.

After listening to what had been happening to him because he stood up for what he believes in, I just sat. He then asked what I thought. Instead of answering right away, I first asked him, "Are you looking for an answer or my opinion?" He opened the door and asked me to give my opinion.

I said, "Dude, you need to shut up. You're only going to get bashed, and you may be worsening the issue, not helping."

He was shocked and replied, "Well, someone's got to stand in the gap!"

I responded, "No, not really. If a gentle answer turns away wrath, then I wonder why your answer is not doing that."

It's because his message wasn't being heard as *gentle*. It came across abrasive, in fact. Maybe he wasn't delivering it in an abrasive way. But today's culture has not only ceased to listen but also hears things differently as well. In a world where everyone is looking for a fight, you have to carefully determine when to speak, when to hush, and when to leave it alone. He might have done better to abide by these words.

> *Do not give what is holy to the dogs; nor cast your pearls before swine, lest they trample them under their feet, and turn and tear you in pieces.* (Matthew 7:6, NKJV)

That's exactly what was happening to him. He based his beliefs on what is holy. The Bible can be seen as his pearls here. But casting them widely into a culture that largely doesn't care to hear it didn't work.

One tool you might use to decide whether to speak is to ask yourself this question first: *Does what I am about to say, HEAL?* What I mean by that is this acronym: Does it **H**elp? Does it **E**ncourage? Does it **A**ffirm? Is it **L**oving? The young man I was speaking to might have the right beliefs, but his comments evidently were not interpreted as helpful, encouraging, affirming, and loving. As such, they did not **HEAL**. While well-meaning, they caused more division, as seen in the directly opposing comments and backlash he received.

I find as I get older, I don't want to argue anymore. If someone says something contrary to what I believe, I just let them think what they want and leave it alone. That doesn't mean I don't defend my beliefs if I am directly asked. It just means I don't butt in where I'm not invited. It also means I think my beliefs stand on their own. I don't think I have to defend them. Why? Because I will win more people with my love and genuine caring for their hearts than I will if I'm known as a big mouth.

If people in this culture aren't listening, your arguments for your beliefs won't be heard. When you spend your time and efforts building relationships instead of a platform, then you can speak of your beliefs when invited to within those close relationships. That's when hearts, spirits, and lives are changed. I love Jesus because He first loved me, not because He came marching in telling me everything I was doing and everything I believed was nuts.

Until there is a place of safety established—relationships where people will listen and allow others to be heard—there's no use in throwing your pearls before swine. You got to know when to hold them, know when to fold them, know when to walk away, and know when to run. That's called wisdom.

At any given time, I live with sixty high school kids from all over the country. They are great kids with great parents who are struggling with some pretty substantial issues and behaviors. The teens need a place away from home to address some of the things going wrong in their lives, so they come to Heartlight for a year to sort through issues, hurts, and struggles. We have faced about anything you can think of that has to deal with inappropriate behavior, wrong thinking, poor choices, and various lifestyles and backgrounds.

> Until there is a place of safety established—relationships where people will listen and allow others to be heard—there's no use in throwing your pearls before swine.

Parents send their kids to us in hopes we can help their teen and give the parents direction as to how to handle their child differently. Many families also want us to solve their extended family problems that have been around for years. That isn't our battle in the war for their teen's heart and life.

Under the banners of standing for what's right, seeking justice, and fighting the good fight, many come to a point where anything opposed to what they believe is grounds for battle. At the very least, many people seem to want to grapple until others understand where they stand.

Many parents go to sleep at night feeling they did what is right in the eyes of the Lord when they stood up against their kids. They mistakenly believe it's a good thing when they let their teen children know what is right and what is wrong. They never realize what they are truly doing is alienating their kids, not only from them but also, often, from the truths they are trying to communicate. By wielding verbal swords, some parents cut their kids down and keep their kids from being positively influenced by them in the future.

Doing what is right in the eyes of the Lord doesn't mean you have to argue anything contrary to Scripture. Please hear me carefully here. You should honor God in all that you do. I'm not encouraging you to give up your beliefs for the sake of a better relationship with your children. I am encouraging more forward thinking. Think through the impact of what you might argue for or against. Then determine whether the argument will deepen your special relationship. You both need a close and loving bond. Will your stance threaten that? If it will, then don't lose your position over an argument that will never be settled peacefully.

> Doing what is right in the eyes of the Lord doesn't mean you have to argue anything contrary to Scripture.

I want to be a lifter of burdens for my grandkids, not one who places more on them.

By the time they are teens, they know the difference between right and wrong. They know what Scripture has to say about certain issues. I can remind them of what they know through encouragement in a much better way than I can through criticism, accusation, or argument. It's not my role to fight with them. It's my role to be a sounding board for them. They talk; I listen. I ask if they want input. If they say no, I honor that and stand by them as they figure it out the right way or the hard way. When they make good choices, I rejoice with them. When they make wrong turns, I hurt with them and for them. I don't control their choices or their beliefs. I couldn't even if I argued 'til I'm blue in the face. I have to learn to button it when I don't agree with it, and just hold my opinions until they're invited.

That's tough sometimes. I'll admit it. I'm a Texan; a typical Texan who doesn't mind standing for what is right or defending what I believe when challenged. I've even had times when I've encouraged a good fight with a comment like, "Bring it on!" However, I'm careful and wise before I draw a line in the sand and go to battle with my grandkids. I do not want a quick win of a battle that turns into the heartbreaking loss of the war for their love, trust, and special relationship with me.

All teens live in a different world today where differing views are prevalent. How they see issues and how we parents see them may be as different as night and day. I must keep trying to view it from their perspective if I'm going to have any impact.

Just a couple of days ago, I heard from a young lady who is a wonderful friend. However, she wanted to have a conversation with me that had been brewing in her for some time. She wanted to let me know she moved to be with a girl she had fallen in love with. She said, "I'm gay. I love Jesus, and I know that He loves me. I've had to come to terms with that." You know, for some, those are fighting words.

Her comments challenged my thinking and beliefs. Because we have developed a trusted relationship over time, I could have asked her any of the following questions. *How can you think that way? What would Jesus say about your comments? How can you justify what the Bible says about homosexuality? Where does this come from? When did all this begin?*

I didn't ask any of those things. I chose to say only, "Sweetheart, I want you to know this. There's nothing you can do to make me love you more, and there's nothing you can do to make me love you less." In a moment I decided the most important way to engage with this dear friend was to communicate a love for our relationship. I let her know I love her dearly. I chose not to correct her. I believe my role is to love. Let the conviction of the Holy Spirit do the correcting. Let the consequences of her choices correct her path. Those life choices, the lifestyle she is embracing, are between her and God.

Saddleback Church Pastor Rick Warren, the author of the best-selling *The Purpose-Driven Life*, once stated,

> Our culture has accepted two huge lies. The first is that if you disagree with someone's lifestyle, you must fear or hate them. The second is that to love someone means you agree with everything they believe or do. Both are nonsense. You don't have to compromise convictions to be compassionate.

Don't compromise your convictions. But make sure your discussions are filled with compassion, as you avoid arguments and create an atmosphere of communication that allows for differences of opinion. Those are tough places for your kids to find. Jesus said, "Come to me and I will give you rest" (Matthew 11:28). Be like Jesus to your kids. Offer them a place of safety and rest, not argument and rejection. If you do, when life gets too tough to handle, they'll run to you.

CHAPTER 17

Quit Correcting and Start Connecting

Let us think of ways to motivate one another to acts of love and good works.

Hebrews 10:24 (NLT)

If I spend all my time correcting everything wrong with the kids living with us at Heartlight, I won't have any time left for the relationships God desires for me to have with them. No one can get everything right all the time.

You may see a lot of things wrong with your kids. They may get on your last nerves and bring out all your pet peeves. Does any of this sound familiar? They make messes, and we have to clean up after them. Rarely do they help with dishes. They don't sit in chairs correctly. They spend too much time on their phones. They play too many stupid games on the iPads and computers. They lounge around and don't offer to help much with any chores. They don't eat the right things. They park their car in the wrong places. They scrounge around for food, eating my special desserts. They never wash the sheets; much less make their beds before they leave. They track in dirt, clog the drains, leave dirty towels lying around, and run up the electric bill. They dig through my stuff and use whatever they want without asking.

My kids' sloppiness may feel like bad manners to me, but do I correct them? Nope. I let it go because I know I need to spend less of our time together correcting and focus my time with them on connecting. The goal of the relationship that you have with your teen needs to be more about "connecting" than "correcting."

In my seminars for parents of teenagers, I somewhat jokingly tell parents to correct teens only on Mondays, Wednesdays, and Fridays. Give them a break from a culture that is always telling them what they do wrong, how they can do it better, and what they need to do differently next time. I encourage parents to correct, but also to give breaks from correction in the hope that they can create a place of rest for their adolescent children. See, correction may change surface behavior. *Connecting* changes the heart.

Speak the language of their heart, not just words to change or stop behaviors. Stop correcting and start connecting.

I encourage parents to spend more time connecting and grandparents not to correct their grandkids at all. Not at all? Am I crazy? I don't think so. Sure, there are things that bug me about my grandkids. However, short of violating the hard-and-fast rules Jan and I have for our home (listed in Chapter 10), we don't correct the grandkids when they visit. Why? Because correction is their parents' job. I believe it's a better strategy for grandparents to give their grandkids a break. Focus on connection with them in ways that build your special relationship. Eventually, they'll do better about their messes because they care about you. (It may take years. Be patient.)

My wife Jan and I have learned to tolerate our grandchildren's inadequacies and sacrifice some of our desires to create an atmosphere where they get a break from the culture they live in every day.

If your coworkers, boss, and customers began to correct you the minute you walked in the door of work every day, you'd quit in a heartbeat. You would not stay long in an atmosphere of constant texts, comments, posts, discussions, and judgments against you. Very few teens survive with their hearts, spirits, and attitudes intact in a world of constant correction.

If your son puts in a good day's work mowing your yard, and the first thing you notice is the patch of grass he missed, I guarantee he won't be back to mow again if he can help it. Even if they are true, refrain from comments that his performance wasn't near as good as you hoped, that he mowed it all wrong, or that he didn't quite finish what he started. Those complaints turn his willingness to help into failure. He wasn't good enough. He didn't meet your exacting expectations.

Again, I believe in teaching kids to do a good job. I want kids to experience the benefits of good hard work. But as a grandparent, I don't correct their efforts when they make them. I want them to show up again and keep learning and trying, and then, over a period of time they'll learn the lesson I want for them, and I'll have a connection that will last a lifetime.

If your sixteen-year-old daughter walks downstairs to breakfast and you don't think she is properly dressed, I'd encourage you to stay away from immediately trying to improve her appearance. Button your lips and don't deliver a message on being modest. If she feels criticized or corrected, she won't be back. You could lose a lifetime of influence in a moment of correction. It's not worth it.

Don't let their behavior get in the way of your special relationship. See the good in them even when it costs you. Speak the language of their heart, not just words to change or stop behaviors. Stop correcting and start connecting.

Understanding Their Behavior

I know I've already said this, but it bears repeating. Please don't let your kids' displeasing behavior push you away. No matter what they are doing or not doing, love them through it. Even if it feels like what they're doing is breaking your heart, be the one person who sticks by them. I deal with kids who are struggling, and the tendency for parents is to try to manage their child's behavior. In some ways, parents have to do that. Their children are their responsibility. But behavior management can put a wedge between parents and kids that keep them from getting to the heart of the real issues that are driving the inappropriate actions.

A wise parent will see beyond the behavior and engage in a way that speaks to their teen's heart.

Behavior is goal-oriented. Whatever your teen is doing, she is doing it for a reason. There is a method to her madness. There is intention in your son's bad behavior. Your kids' behavior is a visible expression of the invisible issues within. A wise parent will see beyond the behavior and engage in a way that speaks to their teen's heart. Parents should not try to manage their children's actions. You can help with heart issues by asking questions that help them get to the root of their conduct. If you've done a good job creating a place of rest and a haven of wisdom, your teens can feel safe sharing what is really going on. This gives you a chance to speak to their deeper internal struggles.

Here are some questions you can ask to get beyond behavior and target the heart:

- Hey, Bud, tell me what's really going on?
- Sweetie, I can see that there's a little bit of conflict. Anything I can help with?
- Do you think the behavior I see might be connected to something I don't see? What am I not seeing?
- If you could change one thing in your life at the snap of your fingers, what would that be?
- Man, that sounds like a mess. Is there any way I can help in all of this?

- Help me understand what you're thinking. I'm a little confused.
- Hey, how's life in the dark hole? Maybe I can help you find a way out.
- Your words say one thing, but I feel like your behavior says something completely different. Help me identify the difference.

Asking the right question at the right time is an amazing way of opening the door to your child's heart, especially when their answer doesn't invoke a consequence or a form of discipline.

Speaking the Language That Touches Their Heart

In 1995, Dr. Gary Chapman wrote a wonderful book called *The Five Love Languages: How to Express Heartfelt Commitment to Your Mate*. This book continues to hit the bestseller lists for more than twenty years since it was first published. It's that good. It contains simple truths that are so profound. The book outlines five ways to express and experience love that Chapman calls *love languages*. These five languages are the giving of gifts, quality time, words of affirmation, acts of service, and physical touch.

This book was written for marriages, yet many parents have applied the same love language tests to their teens, thinking if they learn how their children receives love, they can better meet their needs.

Not long ago, I was a guest on Gary's *Building Relationships* radio program, a great show produced by Moody Radio. I remember asking him if he thought there were more than five love languages. I don't remember his answer, but it did get me thinking.

Years ago we thought there were just nine planets in our solar system. That's what I had learned growing up. That's pretty much the way it was. As young students, we all learned their names by heart and made many mobiles out of coat hangers and Styrofoam balls, painted various colors. We made posters and shoebox dioramas of our massive solar system for science projects through my junior high school years.

The great mystery of our time was the planet Pluto that was discovered in 1930. Scientists argued for years over whether it was a planet or not, much like the argument about whether the Beatles' Paul McCartney was indeed the Walrus and possibly died back in the 1970s. Then something happened in the early 1990s. The first extra-solar planet was discovered, a planet outside of our solar system that orbits a star. What did experts name it? *51 Pegasi B*. It was discovered the same year Gary Chapman's book was published.

Do you want to know how many extra-solar planets have been discovered since that first one? 3,498. That's right. We thought there were just nine, and now we know of 3,500. Amazing, isn't it? The number of planets is far beyond what we could have ever imagined.

I thought if we believed for so long there were just nine planets (Pluto sometimes in, sometimes out), and now there are 3,498, there must be a possibility that when we thought there were just five love languages, there might be a couple more.

I knew there had to be other love languages because those written by Gary never really applied to me. I don't want more gifts, because I've got too much stuff already. I don't want quality time, because I don't have any more time to give. Words of affirmation feel more like people blowing smoke in my ear (flattery) than real encouragement. I don't want anyone to perform an act of service for me like mowing my grass. I can do that myself or hire someone I trust. Finally, I don't want anyone to touch me.

Just because those love languages don't fit me doesn't mean they're not true. Of course, they are. I think I'm the odd duck here. How do I feel loved? I spent the next few months thinking about what other love languages might be. Eventually, I came up with a few that touched my heart. I believe these apply to teens everywhere. Here are two additional ways a parent can express love to their adolescent children.

1. *Defend the ones you love. Show your loyalty.* When teens are wronged, they long to have someone rise above the rest and

defend them. It affirms a sense of loyalty and commitment to your relationship. It proves you are a high priority in each other's life. A teen desires to know he is loved when all is well. He also wants to know he is loved when things aren't so well when peers and others turn against him for whatever reason, even if he's wrong. Your kids want to know that when others are against them, you will be for them, speak up for them if need be, and stand by their side. When you listen to them complain about relationships, don't take the other person's side, even if your teen is wrong. Over time, most issues will work themselves out and your teens will remember how you listened. Show them your loyalty, and they'll feel loved.

2. *An invitation to participate.* Most kids want to be invited to participate, even though they might not attend whatever they've been invited to. I'm the same way. I hate to be left out; just don't expect me to show up when you extend the invitation. I think that I want to be included just as much as teens want to belong. They're desperate to know they are wanted. They want to fit in, long to be popular, desire to be admired. The hardest thing for any teen is to feel left out, excluded, or forgotten about. That's why they're on their phones so much. They don't want to miss anything.

When you defend your child who has been offended, you open the door for a lifelong relationship. When you invite your children to join you, you build a relationship. They will not forget your loyalty or the time you spent with them.

When the Connection Just Isn't Happening

If you're working hard to make a connection and it just doesn't seem to be working, the first thing you must do is ask them some questions. The first question is this simple one: "What am I doing that is keeping us from connecting?" Flat out ask the question. Send it in a text. Tell your teen you'd like to talk about it at some point. Get to the real answer. It may be something you do. It may be something you are saying. They may be embarrassed by your comments. They may think you're goofy. It may be one of your mannerisms that just bugs them. It may be how you treat their friends.

Ask the question. Then give them room to answer any way they want. You don't get to defend yourself or question their answer. The issue is not that you are doing something wrong or inappropriate. The focus of the question

The best of intentions can be perceived completely different. If those good-hearted, intentional acts are getting in the way of a relationship, by all means, stop.

is to see how you can get past whatever it is that is keeping them from making a connection with you. One of our girls at Heartlight came up to me at one of our family retreats and asked me if I would talk to her mom. She said, "Mark, would you talk to my mother and tell her to quit sending me Scripture and all her words of encouragement? They make me feel judged, like she just wants to correct me all the time."

In this case, the daughter interpreted a positive, encouraging act done by a parent as something different. In time, this young lady will welcome her mother's words of encouragement, but for now, she wanted no part of them. The best thing for this mother would be to quit texting and wait for a better time to speak in a language her daughter could take correctly. The best of intentions can be perceived completely different. If those good-hearted, intentional acts are getting in the way of a relationship, by all means, stop.

I don't think I've ever read anything about correction being a love language. You can either choose to *correct* their behavior, which is a temporary fix or, you can *connect* for a lifetime. What do you think your children really want?

CHAPTER  18

Giving Your Teen Control of Their Life

Start children off on the way they should go, and even when
they are old they will not turn from it.

Proverbs 22:6

Hey, who wants to have a twenty-five-year-old clown, lounge lizard, or son hanging around the house playing video games? And who of you really wants your daughter to "get lost" and make quick decisions that are going to affect her the rest of her life, just because she didn't know how to take control of her life?

So, if you have total control of your child at age twelve, and you want them to have total control of their life at age eighteen, then you must start turning that control over to them, little-by-little, year-by-year. Agreed? Would you also agree that you must start letting them make some of their own decisions, so they're capable of doing the same when they graduate from high school? And would you agree with me that, in the process of learning discernment and seeing the need to make wise decisions, there will be a few hiccups along the way?

It's a scary process, isn't it? Every part of us, as parents, wants to protect and keep our children out of harm's way. But in reality, the exercise of their decision-making muscles is the only way they'll learn. It's imperative that we allow them to make decisions and reap the benefits, or suffer the consequences along the way. Remember, if we transfer this process over a seven-year period and year-by-year, this type of transition gives them more opportunities to take successful control of their life.

Every parent knows the main issue of turning over control is taking a risk that some mistakes will be made. But if that parent also knows that all mistakes and choices have consequences, they can view errors and slip-ups as a gaining of experience that will only benefit teens on their next decision-making go-around.

It's imperative that we allow our teens to make decisions and reap the benefits, or suffer the consequences along the way.

Here are some decisions that we can transfer to them between twelve and eighteen years of age (twelve being the age that you have full control of their lives). The years before they reach eighteen are the transition years. This time is where you turn over your rights, in hopes of them accepting their responsibilities.

Did you dress the way that your parents dressed? Did you really have a longing desire to look like your mom or dad did when they were in high school? Then what makes you think your teens want to dress like you, much less, feel like you know how they should dress? Let them start making these choices. The parental fear is that they'll make some poor choices and show too much cleavage, wear something too tight or too loose, or expose too much skin, right? Let school officials hold to their rules and send your teens home if they are inappropriate. Allow a boss at work to let your children know what is proper and suitable. Let other kids around your teen express their opinion on how they appear. They'll learn over a period of time. Once your children head out of the home at eighteen, they'll know how to dress accordingly.

Did your parents monitor every phone call and note you wrote to friends when you were seventeen? Of course not! On the contrary, today's parents have this desire to monitor every Internet history and viewing, which is driven by a fear that they may be looking at something inappropriate or motivated by worry that they're going be stalked by a predator. I can assure you of this, if you have taught your teens through the years how to handle the Internet, with all its pornography, lies, and half-truths, then the chances of them making poor decisions are a lot less than if you maintain control in this area of their lives.

Hey, helping and even doing their fifth-grade science project, which is really a middle school competition among dads, is an okay thing. But doing all their work for them when they're seventeen years old isn't okay. If you are still having to push and pull to get your child to complete academics at this age, then your child will fail when they head off to the "big school," or have some serious lessons to learn when they enter the armed services or get a job. Let them do it, and let them suffer the consequences of not doing it. It's far better for them to flunk a class now, on their own. They'll have to go to summer school to learn they might need to take responsibility to study a bit more in the future.

At age twelve, you, as a parent, choose whom they hang out with or not. At age eighteen, it's their deal. If you have an eighteen-year-old at home and you have picked all their friends through their adolescent years, they won't know what to do or have the ability to make good peer selection during their first year away from home (unless you plan on tagging along with them and be their social coordinator). Let them start making choices.

During middle school, you should have a program of spiritual education for them. And by the age of eighteen, they should be able to make all their choices regarding their learning about the Lord. At age sixteen, you may want to require them to go to church, but they get to choose where they go. At age seventeen, you may want to let them decide whether they go or not. If they choose not to go, still invite them to come eat lunch with you after you go to church.

Let me add a couple of points on this one. First, if your children rebel against your rules and boundaries at home, what do you think will be the first point of conflict (where they show you they want control of their life)? It's church participation. Because church participation is dear to you, they will use it and attack your greatest passion for proving they are in control. Give it to them. Take the *church card* off the table, and let them make decisions, and they can never use it against you to communicate a message.

Second, if you're reading this thinking, "*As for me and my house, we will serve the Lord,*" and "*As long as you're living in my house, you'll go to church,*" remember, in a very short while, they'll be able to make their own decisions. And that which is presented to them in an authoritarian style (as mentioned earlier), they'll walk away from. Be careful with this approach. I see that it doesn't bode too well with teens today.

Whoever started this concept that kids aren't supposed to date because they kissed dating goodbye, didn't know teens. The dating process gives an opportunity for your teen to learn how to select who they will spend the rest of their life with. It will provide them with the opportunity to determine what kind of person they "gel" with. Look, my wife and I dated since we were fourteen and did so for six years before we got married. Wonderful experience. So, let them start making some decisions at some determined age. My concern for this group of today's teens is that they don't date, they hang out in groups because they haven't learned how to socially engage in such a way that they feel competent to be alone with someone of the opposite sex. That's scary for me.

Finally, I know there are movies and a ton of music that doesn't stand up to the biblical standards that I hold. Quite frankly, most of the world I see doesn't hold up to those standards. And your teen is living smack dab in the middle of it. They've heard things we never heard, been exposed to so much more than we could have ever imagined, and seen things I would have never thought would be on a movie screen. The age of permissiveness, promotion, and presentation is rampant when it comes to what our teen's experience. Having said that, it's all the more reason to help them make good choices. I would encourage you to spend time transferring the opportunity to choose what they want to see and listen to, so they're ready to make good decisions when they leave your home.

Hey, there's risk in everything. Right? And when we give over responsibility to our kids to make decisions in their lives, we're taking a risk. It's just that not handing over responsibility and control has greater consequences. John Maxwell said, "Everything in life brings risk. It's true that you risk failure if you try something bold because you might

The age of permissiveness, promotion, and presentation is rampant when it comes to what our teen's experience.

miss it. But you also risk failure if you stand still and don't try anything new."

Who in the world really thinks handing the keys to the family car to a sixteen-year-old and giving them the opportunity to drive around Los Angeles, Dallas, Chicago, Philadelphia, or Miami is a good idea? Quite honestly, it sounds like a stupid idea. But we do it. And to all of our surprise, teens begin to learn the need to make wise choices, and they "step up to the plate" and swing and many times "hit it out of the park." There's always a risk! There's a risk every time your teens walk out the door and sit down behind the steering wheel of a car or get into a car with someone else.

If you're moving from a teaching model to a training model, there's risk. The risk of making poor decisions while transferring and building stronger decision-making muscles causes far less damage than not giving your children any chance at all to take control of their lives.

The greater risk is when you are still determining what they are wearing, monitoring their Internet access, overseeing their academics, picking their friends, forcing them to go to church, determining who they date, and still selecting their movies, music, and which social networking site they can access. This is a surefire promise that your children will fail when they turn eighteen. That, my friend, would be a mess and a disaster waiting to happen. And this is not an exhaustive list!

I can tell by the way you're reading these words that you're wincing a bit. I can tell this is one area that is hard for you. You know what? It should be. You must be intentional about what you do and not give all decision-making opportunity to your teen without some careful and thoughtful process.

The reason I do it, as a parent, is to shift from a "teaching mode" to a "training mode" to see if all the stuff I've *taught* has been *caught*. It's a slow and sometimes painful process, and there will always be a few hiccups along the way, but it is imperative in helping my teen move into adulthood.

Here's my point. Many times, teens will hold on to something (like all the music we would rather them not listen to) just to prove to us that they are in control. As a parent, I don't want a child holding on to something that I don't really approve of, just to prove he or she is in control. Follow me?

Eliminate the phrase "I told you so" from your vocabulary; it accomplishes nothing except *shaming* your teen and only pushes them further into sin.

You must give teens the opportunity to make decisions and develop their decision-making muscle because, in the long run, their ability to make good decisions will far outweigh any impact some offensive music will have on them.

Make sure that consequences are detailed so that your child understands the need to be wise and make good decisions. Wisdom brings pleasure and foolishness brings pain. And when your teens make a poor choice, not just a mistake that most teens make because they're adolescents, make sure they *feel* the consequence.

If your teen gets a DUI, then help him/her learn the process, pay whatever fine, and accept whatever consequences arise. If your teen flunks a class, let him/her learn the need to study and take responsibility. If your child gets arrested or in trouble for being disrespectful, let him/her learn and suffer the consequences, both legally and financially. The same goes for a speeding ticket. If your teen gets kicked off of a sports team for an infraction, use it as an opportunity for him/ her to learn about making good and wise choices. Let consequences have their full effect. Don't rescue them! Proverbs 19:19 clearly states, "*If you rescue an angry man once, you'll just have to rescue them again.*"

The process of transferring control is a perfect example of what discipline really is. Discipline is helping your teens get to where they want to go and keeping them from where they don't want to end up. It's about them. Let them make decisions. Let them choose. Let them learn from their mistakes, and help them understand that they are responsible for their lives… not you. We're helping them take control of their life, rather than fighting them for it.

When your teens make a mistake, don't ridicule them for their choices. Be calm and accepting when they get sent home from school for wearing something the school deems inappropriate. They can learn from others. Eliminate the phrase "I told you so" from your vocabulary; it accomplishes nothing except *shaming* your teen and only pushes them further into sin.

Trust what you've taught them and trust that God is involved in their lives. Help them with their decisions, and give them the opportunity to let God be more involved.

I want teens to have the opportunity to make mistakes and have parents present in their lives when that happens. Speak truth into their life amidst the issue, instead of postponing their learning to a later time, when you aren't around to offer good sound advice and guidance. You have to choose whether you're going to raise your teens to live in the zoo or train them to survive in the jungle. Your teens would desire for you to choose the latter, as they will be better prepared to meet life's challenges and become healthy adults.

Give up control, so your teens can take control. And when they make mistakes along the way, and they will, be there for them to speak wisdom into their lives. They will begin to learn and embrace the need to search out wisdom before making key decisions that will affect them the rest of their lives.

Kids who learn to make good decisions do so at the risk of making some poor ones. However, they gather experience and wisdom from the lessons learned from both. Christian parents, for the most part, are too protective and sometimes overly involved, to the point of not allowing kids to grow up. Let go. Trust what you've been teaching them and give your teens that opportunity to grow and learn…the same way that you did.

CHAPTER 19

Complaining Ruins Relationships; Gratefulness Draws Them In

When you talk, don't say anything bad. But say the good things that people need—whatever will help them grow stronger. Then what you say will be a blessing to those who hear you.

Ephesians 4:29 (ERV)

As the years pass quicker and quicker, we begin to see the unavoidable aging process. We can't help but notice the downward gravitational pull on our bodies. It's inevitable. It's foreseeable. It's certain. We're getting older. The inescapable reality of our fate is that one day we will be gone. What will remain are the memories of who we were. Most won't remember all the things we said, but they will remember how we made them feel. My prayer is that I never make anyone feel uncomfortable around me. So, I've made some choices.

Because I don't want to get fat, I work out to make sure I stay in shape the best I can. Because I love good health, I watch what I eat. Because I don't want to break anything, I watch the activities I engage in. Because I don't want two earfuls of hair, age spots all over my face, shriveled and damaged hands, and veins road-mapping my nose, I choose dermatology procedures to keep that from happening. There are choices I can make so my life will be better longer, and there are some things that just aren't under my control.

You know what I want more than anything else? I want to be a grandpa who is grateful for what and who I have in my life. What I don't want to be is a cantankerous old man who is bitter and broken because life didn't turn out the way I planned. I know this for sure. My wife doesn't want to become a cranky old woman who rants and raves about everything. I can't imagine a Jan who expresses disappointment that life should have treated her better. I know my wife wants to be grateful and thankful for each day God gives her. She is.

These desires go hand-in-hand with the choices we make. Short of developing dementia or losing your physical health, you can choose whether you'll be a cranky ol' woman or that cantankerous ol' man. As long as you have your faculties, you have a choice. That choice determines whether your legacy is a positive one to be remembered or a negative one, hopefully quickly forgotten.

I'm not sure people actually realize how they come across. I'm sure most folks prefer to be seen as good-natured. I haven't met anyone who truly wants family, friends, and strangers alike to avoid them. However, many parents don't know just how their kids see them. I interviewed a number of teens and asked them to tell me about their parents. Some of their answers were not complimentary. Most were just sad. Here's how they described some of their parents:

- Very bitter about everything.
- Full of disappointment.
- Argues about everything; is just looking for a fight.
- Has become crabby and disagreeable.
- Judgmental attitude toward everything.
- Opinionated, with outbursts full of gripes or criticisms.
- Complains about everything.

- Unreasonable, belligerent, and grouchy.
- Never shuts up.

With some degree of certainty, I'm pretty sure I've never met a parent who said, "You know, I sure would like to be like..." any one of the statements I just listed. But it happens. When parents wonder why their kids don't want to be in their presence, it baffles me how many don't have a clue why they are being avoided.

Let me ask you something. Would you really like to hang around someone who displays any of the characteristics on that list? I wouldn't. While I say that, I'm scared to death I might unknowingly be like or become like the things on that list.

Here are a couple of things you can do to find out if you have become an offensive person who is to be avoided. Ask God to search your heart. Psalm 139:23-24 says,

Search me, God, and know my heart; test me and know my anxious thoughts. See if there is any offensive way in me, and lead me in the way everlasting.

You can pray for God to reveal what it is in you that is pushing your children away. It may be the very thing your spouse has said for years. Perhaps co-workers or bosses said it to you or about you. I'm sure you know there's some truth in the harder words that have come your way through various people all your life. Your relationships and your legacy hang in the balance here. It's time to deal with those unpleasant ways you've developed, so you can ensure your legacy is one to be remembered, not one to be quickly forgotten.

Ask your kids. If you're afraid to ask your kids how they see you, that's a good indicator you might have some areas to work on. Text them and try it. Pure and simple, you know kids will say things in texts they wouldn't say

191

face-to-face. So ask them. Text them these questions, "What is it that makes you want to avoid me? What am I doing to push you away, because that's not what I want to do?" If they text back, "You complain and gripe about everything," don't rush to explain, excuse, or justify. Accept their words, tell them thanks for sharing, and begin to change. Even at your age, you can make new habits, especially if the old ones are getting between you and your kids. No one likes a complainer or grumbler, one who is discontent with his lot in life. Remember Philippians 2:14? Do everything without complaining and arguing.

Most teens avoid constant complainers, including parents, like the plague. They live in this culture of negativity all the time. If that's what they're going to get from Mom and Dad too, they will look elsewhere for their encouragement and assurance of hope. There isn't any hope to be found in one who complains all the time.

> Most teens avoid constant complainers, including parents, like the plague.

I've met many people aging with a great deal of anger, unhappy that life didn't turn out the way they had hoped, critical of folks and God because they feel abandoned. If life is now a half-empty glass, these folks look at the empty portion all the time. They focus all their remaining energies on their losses and disappointments. These are reflected in their words, actions, and constant rants about how life would have been different if they were dealt a different set of cards to play. Their words already speak death, not a grateful heart and a hope of heaven to come.

I recently talked to a friend I've known for forty years. He began to speak of an incident that happened to him thirty-eight years ago. His discussion centered on how his life would have been so different if the pastor of the church he worked for almost four decades before had treated him differently. The discussion wasn't just a few sentences of disgust or disappointment. It lasted for forty-five minutes! This friend spent thirty-eight years rolling the scenario of disappointment around in his head, justifying his own loss, blaming someone else, and expressing his disappointment in life through his words and comments.

Disappointment in life comes out as anger. Anger and unforgiveness dig roots of bitterness and resentment, which foster arguments, fighting, crabbiness, judgmental tendencies, disagreeableness, opinionated harping, as well as complaining, griping, being grouchy, and unreasonable. Anger and unforgiveness never offer hope.

There are some battlefields where wars continue to be fought, even though the enemy is long gone. Those are the battlefields of your mind and your emotions. If you find yourself stuck, it will pour out on those around you. If you know there are things from the past you can't get passed, it's time to get some help in the form of counseling and therapy. It is well worth the time and effort to become healthy. Then you can be a testimony of forgiveness, an example of healing and wholeness, and a beacon of hope to your children. I do believe you can teach an old dog new tricks. It's never too late to mend fences, and one is never too old to change his ways.

Gratefulness

Remember earlier in the book when I mentioned that one of the jobs of a parent is to give perspective? Here's a hopeful story I offer to anyone who has experienced disappointment and loss in their life. I had high expectations for a particular fellow in my life. As the years passed, I found I grew angrier and angrier with him. I expected him to be something he never was. I wanted him to give me things he never gave. Every time I saw him I thought about how he hurt and upset me by failing to meet my expectations and give me opportunities to forge a deeper relationship with him. I was angry for years—that quiet kind of anger that simmers continuously, but it never really spews over to anyone else. I just felt a sting whenever I thought about this person. Ever had anger like that?

Then I had a dream. I dreamed I died and went to heaven. As I approached God, I noticed this person, the object of my years of anger, was standing next to Him as I was ushered into His presence. My anger boiled over. I was mad that this person was standing next to God after continually disappointing me. I expressed my feelings to God, using some words I was shocked I would say to Him even in a dream. God quickly stopped me. He

Regardless of your current circumstances, if you are grateful, that's a legacy that will be talked about long after you're gone.

answered with a short remark that changed my life. He said, "Mark, I want you to know something. I've been using this person in your life to mold you into the person I wanted you to be." You know, that's all I needed to hear to understand why that happened in my life. Since that dream, I have felt no anger towards this person at all.

What I thought was so bad was really a good thing. It's all about perspective. Because of my God-given new perspective, I'm not angry. Instead, I became extremely grateful for my circumstances. It's just sad that it took me until I was in my fifties before I realized what He was doing.

A heart full of gratefulness leaves no room for complaining. There's just something about a thankful person that is attractive and appealing. It's as simple as this. Every time I cook a meal at our home when my granddaughter Macie comes over to eat, she always—I mean always—says, "Thanks for dinner, Poppa." That is a simple comment, but it moves me every time. Her gratitude expressed in just those four words makes me want to cook every meal for her and make it the best it can be.

I know what I don't want to become in my older years. Ungrateful. I know exactly what I want for my all my family as they grow older—hope and gratefulness. I want them to be chock-full of hope and crammed with gratefulness for the life before them. I want them to know that whatever they face, they can get through it. If you complain and are ungrateful for where you are in life, it speaks volumes to teens that feel like they sometimes can't make it through the next week.

Regardless of your current circumstances, if you are grateful for who you are, what you have, and whom you have in your life, that's a legacy that will be talked about long after you're gone. When you have hope, your children start to believe they can make it too. When they are overwhelmed, your joy and grateful heart can restore and refuel them. Because of what they see and hear from you, they believe they can move past tough situations. It also puts life into better perspective for teens; it tells them their hard days will pass. They will mess up, blow it, and let people down. Other people they count on will mess up, blow it, and let them down. Still, hope can prevail because they have seen you get through similar or worse situations.

Weeping may last through the night, but joy comes with the morning. (Psalm 30:5, NLT)

My dear friend Chelsea Cameron has been a guest on our radio show for years. Her words are impactful, and her message touches hearts as she shares her views on parenting. The most profound comment I've heard from her is the message she wants to communicate to her kids. "On our best of days, and our worst of days, I want you to know that our family is better because you are in it." Wow! What a message to convey to a tired and weary teen searching for significance and security. What hope to offer a kid who longs to belong to a family that will never quit on him!

Okay, Mom and Dad, now you have a choice. Do you want to be a cantankerous ol' man or cranky ol' woman? Or would you rather be a parent full of hope, one who is grateful for God's presence in your life?

It's your choice. Choose wisely, my friend.

CHAPTER  20

Can Everyone Just Laugh a Little?

*A cheerful heart is good medicine, but a crushed spirit dries up
the bones.*

Proverbs 17:22

When we started our *Parenting Today's Teens* radio program ten
years ago, we traveled the country peddling our program to radio
stations everywhere. We hoped they would pick it up and give us a chance
to prove that parents and grandparents were searching for help and hope in
raising teens. We relentlessly pursued these stations. Radio programmers
did not want to take a chance. They had no idea who I was.

To them, I came out of left field, starting a radio broadcast at age
fifty-two. I had no previous history of recording or even an understanding of
how to get people to carry our program. When this guy in jeans and boots,
with a mustache from the nineteenth century, strolled into radio stations,
programmers had not seen anything like it before. Add the fact that I wanted
to do a program about dealing with teens, and that was a curveball for most.

Nevertheless, some gave us a chance. Now many stations air our
program, and it does well. We are thrilled to partner with so many wonderful
radio stations throughout North America. One organization asked if they

could test the waters first. They wanted to see how I do while *on mic* (live on the air). They invited me to come in and do a drive-time program on a Tuesday morning from six to eight o'clock. The first hour would be me talking with the morning show host. The second hour would be me answering calls from the listening audience. Our radio team thought this would be a great opportunity to show who we were and give the radio station and their audience a taste of what we were all about. We decided to go, in hopes of them carrying our program.

Well, the day before I was to go on-air with this station, a national scandal broke about a pastor. This pastor, who had been very anti-homosexual in his preaching and critical of the gay lifestyle, had made headlines once before when he got caught in a homosexual relationship exposed by his partner. Now, this pastor was in the national news again. The new story proclaimed the pastor was one hundred percent heterosexual after going through counseling. Many news sources covered the story.

It was a big story when he was exposed; it was now bigger news that he had been restored in his relationship with his family. Again, this story broke the day before my trial run on this radio group, a group that was pretty conservative. Okay, it was very conservative. Anyway, we got to the studio early the next day, and our radio producer and good friend Roger looked at me and said, "Okay, Mark, now don't blow it!" The radio station's people all gathered to watch the guy with the mustache and to make a determination about carrying our program. I was on one side of the glass booth with the morning show host. Everyone else was on the other side, observing while sipping coffee.

The show began. For the first hour, I answered questions, had a great conversation about teens, and discussed the needs of adolescents. I told parents how they could counter the effects this contrary culture was having on their family. Everyone on the other side of the glass smiled, loved the interaction, and gave winks or nods at key moments to let me know of their approval.

Then the second hour began. The host opened up the phone lines to take a few questions from the listening audience. Guess what the first question was? It was a young lady who said, "Mark, I have a question for you. Are you one hundred percent heterosexual?" The folks on the other side of the glass slowly lowered their coffee cups in anticipation of my answer. Our producer Roger crossed his arms, then held his head in his hands. He rubbed his forehead and didn't even look up. I answered, "You know, I don't think so." One would have thought I just stated the Pope isn't Catholic. Birds

If you don't lighten up, you'll never be able to discuss the hard issues with teens or their parents.

quit chirping, all traffic stopped, and the radio folks gasped when I made this comment. "You know, I don't think so," I repeated. "I think I'm ninety-five percent heterosexual, three percent metrosexual because I wear Tommy Bahama shirts occasionally, and two percent homosexual because I'd kiss Keith Urban if I had a chance." (Keith Urban is a country singer married to actress Nicole Kidman. I've been a fan for years.) I thought it was the perfect answer. Behind the smile on my face, I was belly-laughing, thinking I just hit it out of the park with such a humorous response. The radio guys did not agree.

Immediately, the live show switched to the weatherman sharing the forecast for the day. The next sound I heard was a loud rapping on the window and the producer saying, "You can't say that! YOU CAN'T SAY THAT!" Everybody got very quiet. All you could hear was the weather report droning on in the background. I thought this was a great defining moment for me to let them know who I am. I stood up, looked through the glass at all the radio execs, and simply stated, arms stretched out, "If you guys don't lighten up, you'll never be able to discuss the hard issues with teens or their parents."

Great story, eh? Okay, I embellished a little, but you get my point. Right? You've got to lighten up. So many take everything so seriously that their intended message isn't accepted because of the sourpuss look on the messenger's face.

I was speaking in Duck Dynasty Land last year and told this radio story to a church congregation. They roared with laughter. A seventy-five-year-old lady came up to thank me for my comments afterward. She said, "We haven't laughed like that in this church for twenty-five years!" Then a thirty-year-old guy came up and said, "Mark, you know you can throw a bigger brick if it's wrapped in humor." Here was a young man who got it. My sentiments exactly.

> You can throw a bigger brick if it's wrapped in humor.

Here are a couple of quotes from one of my heroes who evidently thinks like I do:

> If you're not enjoying most of your day, if you've stopped having fun, you're missing more than you are contributing. (Swindoll, 2015)

I'm not encouraging laughing everything off. Nor am I suggesting you make a joke of everything. Good jokes do not make bad things good. Proverbs 25:10 (NLT) states,

> *Singing cheerful songs to a person with a heavy heart is like taking someone's coat in cold weather or pouring vinegar in a wound.*

You have to be careful how you use humor but lightening a heavy moment with humor can make a hard truth easier to digest.

I encourage all types of parents to lighten up a bit. Don't make everything so serious in your approach to your kids. You can talk about some very, very serious issues and still laugh in the middle of those hard discussions. Laughter lets them know your relationship is still intact, no matter how hard the conversation is. Hope is instilled, no matter how tough the situation, because you can still smile. Don't minimize the situation, but don't make it any bigger and heavier than it has to be.

Laughter is a form of worship. It lets everyone hear the confidence you have that God is still in control in the midst of whatever is happening. Your wisdom can be received and perhaps better acknowledged when you don't have a frown on your face.

After living with thousands of teens, I know laughter is greatly needed in kids' lives. Their lives are so heavy. Their poor choices and consequences are sometimes grim. Life has gotten so hard. They need to learn again how to have some innocent fun. There's nothing funny or humorous when a teen is struggling. Truly, there's nothing funny about kids

Don't minimize the situation, but don't make it any bigger and heavier than it has to be.

who have given up hope. But there is a need for fun and laughter to instill a new sense of hope.

When I finally hear laughter from a struggling teen, I know they are on a path to healing. Learning to laugh again becomes an essential part of discovering a renewed sense of hope.

Look for the Humor in Situations

Some of the greatest comedians spend their lives helping us look and laugh at ourselves. It's healthy. We're funny people. Just spend a little time at the mall or an airport, and you'll laugh when you see what a funny-looking and weird-acting species we are. When you laugh, remember people are laughing at you as much as you are laughing at them!

Do you think Jesus and the disciples ever had a good laugh? I mean, a hold-your-belly-crying-tears-can't-get-your-breath laugh that just couldn't stay contained? I think so. Here was a carpenter, a handful of fishermen, a tax collector, and the Lord only knows what everyone else did as an occupation (That's a joke!), and you don't think they laughed and told jokes?

Some of my funniest times in life have been when I'm with other fishermen. We tell stories, joke with one another, and have all kinds of fun catching our next meal. I bet you Jesus and the disciples were even told to keep it down a bit when they visited restaurants and stayed at inns. There is a time for everything, including laughter.

> *A time to weep and a time to laugh, a time to mourn and a time to dance.* (Ecclesiastes 3:4)

Look for Opportunities to Have a Good Belly-Laugh

I recently had dinner with a family. They asked me to come by and spend the evening observing them. The parents wanted ideas to help change the declining relational atmosphere within their home. After an entire evening with the parents and three kids (two were teens), I asked the mom why it was so quiet around the table at dinner. Her response shocked me. She said, "We don't allow any laughter at the dinner table." My comment shocked her. "You've got to be kidding me! That's horrible!" I said. I never heard anyone come right out and say that. However, I've seen it implied in many different family's homes. They're the ones where teens would choose to be elsewhere if they could.

I never limit laughter in my home. When we're all together, I believe it's more important for them to have fun than to sit down and listen to my teaching, lessons, and diatribes about leading a successful and fruitful life. Why? Because if we have some fun and learn to laugh, the doors of their hearts will swing open. Their ears will open to hear what I need to share in the days ahead.

Here are some ways to add fun to your home:

- Watch a funny movie (one *they* think is funny).

- Grab an iPad and try to beat each other in a contest to find the funniest comedian on YouTube.
- Hold a joke night at dinner where everyone has to come to the table with a joke ready to be told. (Then give a prize of twenty dollars for the best joke.)
- Sit around the fireplace and tell the funniest stories you've ever heard.
- Spend time jokingly commenting on past events. Laugh about people's responses.

I like this quote:

I have not seen anyone dying of laughter, but I know millions who are dying because they are not laughing. (Kataria, 2010 Tweet)

Tell a Few Jokes and Give Yourself Permission to Laugh

One of the most serious men I've ever met makes sure he tells no less than three jokes when you are in his presence. It's become his trademark. And he tells the best jokes. Really. No one has an excuse for not being able to find good jokes for any age, as there are millions on the Internet. Why not greet your teens at the door with a joke, saying, "Here, I got a good one for you!"

Give yourself permission not to be so serious all the time. Lighten up a little. Exaggerate your stories a bit to get a good response. Tell a joke to add some humor. Make fun of yourself, so your kids know you can have fun as much as the next guy. Laugh at your own mistakes so your grandkids will know you'll laugh at some of theirs.

Laughter is something that comes from within, reflecting an inner peace and the humility to let go and have a good chuckle. Hey, put a smile back on your face. It's contagious.

CHAPTER  21

You're Kidding Me.
This is Important?

So we fix our eyes not on what is seen, but on what is unseen,
since what is seen is temporary, but what is unseen is eternal.

2 Corinthians 4:18

For the sake of this chapter, let me clarify that what is *important* is usually focused on the here and now, and what is *valuable* has to do with that which will retain future value.

There are many things you wake up to each day that you think are important to complete or finish. Those important and much-needed tasks to complete nag at you until they are finished. They have an amazing way of eating up time, energy, and resources. The same time, energy, and resources could be expended to complete things that are more valuable and longer lasting.

Call it the tyranny of the urgent or exchanging what is valuable for that which is urgent. Important things may be easier or screaming to be handled quickly. The reality is that many important matters take away opportunities for some pretty valuable intentions.

You may think it important to play golf, mow the yard, or spend the weekend working around the house, but what may be more valuable is hanging out with a daughter who just broke up with a boyfriend. That golf course will always be there, and that grass will always keep growing, but your daughter will one day move away.

You may think it important to go fishing with your buddies, but what may be more valuable is taking a child fishing so you all can spend some time together. Your time with your child can change his life, and it's doubtful your buddy's life will change much because you hung out on a boat.

The reality is that many important matters take away opportunities for some pretty valuable intentions.

You may think it important to go on a mission trip on the other side of the world to visit orphans, but what may be more valuable is spending time with your daughter who has been bullied and beaten up by some friends. You can go on a mission trip later. You won't always be able to comfort a hurt little girl who calls you Mom or Dad. You may think it important to do something for others, but what may be more valuable is to do something for your family who hasn't seen you in a while. Others can wait; your family won't.

You may think it important to buy that new flat-panel TV, golf club, gun, or tool for your garage, but it may be more valuable to invest that money in purchasing something for your son, something he will remember forever. You may think it important to host a dinner for friends, but what may be more valuable is to spend time with a daughter who doesn't feel like she has any friends. There's always another meal to eat with your peers, but never another opportunity like this. You may think it important to complete your project, but it may be more valuable to get that ice cream with your teen who just needs some hang time with Mom or Dad.

Maybe baking those cookies with a daughter is the very thing that saves her life...*seriously*! If you don't think so, then you don't understand the power you possess as a parent to bring hope to any situation. What is the most valuable thing you can do for your child? Invest your time. Invest your money. Invest your heart. That's what it will cost you. It's a big price, but the rewards for your involvement will return a hundred-fold to you in the way your family views you now and how they will remember you later.

Here's what I think is valuable in the lives of your children and worthy of your provision:

A Listening Ear

Everyone needs a valued listener, and your kids are no exception. Think about it. Who do they have that will really sit down, listen, and give them a place to vent and spew, complain, and criticize?

A young lady made a hurtful comment to me last week. She got in trouble for being disrespectful to some of our Heartlight staff. I merely said, "Want to hear some advice to get out of this mess?" I thought she would say, "Sure!" or "Yes, please tell me what I need to do." or "I would love to hear what you have to say." Those weren't her comments.

Listening includes a heartfelt desire to get to know the person you're listening to.

She said, "Why would I listen to you? You don't even know who I am!" She was teaching me, once again, a lesson I've heard many, many times before. You can't just listen for the sake of listening. Listening includes a heartfelt desire to get to know the person you're listening to, or they will smell a rat a mile away. Teens know when you have an interest in their lives and want to hear all about them and when you're just listening because that's what a good parent is *supposed* to do. They want someone to listen to them. And they want to be heard by someone who has an interest in them. You can be that person. That's more than important. It's more than valuable. That's invaluable.

Access to Wise Counsel

Sometimes teens need to vent to let out their frustrations. They must vent to someone who will keep private their stupid comments and absurd accusations. They know they're being ridiculous. They're just mad, and they want to get that anger out. You can be a safe place where they can let off some of their steam, without scolding or making fun of what they say.

After their tongues rattle a while, their minds usually kick back in gear and they come to some better conclusions than where they started.

Typical teens learn from their own experiences. Wise teens learn from the experiences of others.

Many times, conversations need to remain between the person talking and the person listening.

Give them time to speak what is on their hearts or stuck in their heads, and they'll either come to some resolution or ask you a question to help them get to one. When you have been this funnel of frustration a number of times, you'll begin to win the right to be heard in the deeper, harder issues your child will eventually bring to the table. I call those *decision-discussions* where they genuinely want to know what you think so they can come to a decision about something on their hearts.

Typical teens learn from their own experiences. Wise teens learn from the experiences of others. Teens can't become wise if they don't have those others they can trust. Parents are in the perfect position to help their teens gain wisdom from their experiences. A parent with a listening ear can move a child to a deeper level, where they know there is always available understanding, compassionate listening, and healthy processing of their emotional turmoil. That's absolutely invaluable.

Affirmation of Who They Are

The way you listen probably sends a greater message of hope than any words that come out of your mouth. Just as you know when someone is preoccupied with some other matter when you are talking, your teen knows the same. Any hint of distraction or disinterest will force your teen to search for another empathetic listening ear. Make sure you give your undivided attention when you sit and listen. Pick a place conducive to listening. Create an atmosphere where you won't be interrupted.

I usually pick a restaurant I know will be quiet. My grandkids know that when I want to sit down and talk with them, we're going to a quiet place, and we're going to sit in the back where interruptions are minimal. I plan it that way, and they expect it. I want them to know they are the most important things in my life when I sit down and open my ears to their hearts.

If you're like most dads, you want to fix any problem they talk about. If you're like most moms, you might want to give ten answers to their problem, with personal scenarios for each. Many times, all teens need is someone to listen. I would encourage you not to try to fix or solve their issues. Just convey hope and tell them how special they are. Remind them of who they are whenever they forget.

You don't have to have an eloquent array of words. Just make them feel they are just as important to you now, sitting across from you in a discussion, as they were the day you first held them in your arms. Assure them they continue to be a blessing to your family, as they were the day they came into this world. Help them remember those who love them, rely on them, and with whom they have some very special and exceptional relationships. Make your teen kids feel valued. This is more than valuable—it's invaluable.

A Refuge from the Storms of Life

Like I stated earlier, as a parent, you can provide a safe place during the storms of your teens' lives. When they are battered by the culture, swing wide the doors of your home and your heart. See the preciousness in the most messed-up, beat-up child of yours. You create an atmosphere of hope and refuge when you listen and accept them right where they are.

Teenagers don't pay attention to you just because you're their parent. They come to you because of what they see in you and how you respond to them in various situations. They come to you because of how they see you treat others. They come because they've heard your compassion, seen your heart, and felt your kindness. They watch and learn even at times when they are not asking you to listen. Based on what they see in you, they will determine how much of a refuge you can be.

The life message to be transferred here is that they can find rest in your presence. With you, they can take a break from the normal busyness of life, and they can find a place of comfort when the storms of life are raging. That's more than valuable—it's invaluable.

Transitioning from Theoretical Truth to Practical Application

One of the most valuable roles a parent plays in the lives of their children is helping them take the theoretical truths they have learned through their formative years and apply them in practical ways. This can be one of the most challenging, but rewarding, aspects of parenting. When they participate in this awakening, moms and dads get to have an amazing impact on the hearts of their kids.

Here's an example. Most kids have heard Romans 8:28, "And we know that in all things God works for the good of those who love him, who have been called according to his purpose." They've heard it a million times, right? In one sense, it is theoretical truth for them until there comes a time for practical application.

That happens with a loss or a quick turn of events that changes the direction of a family. It might be a disaster, a catastrophe, or a hard-to-understand act of violence. It might even be a personal failure. In these situations, teens need the wisdom of their parents to help them understand and comprehend what that particular Scripture really means.

This transition of truth to an application isn't just accepted. It is transferred. It's something valuable that can only be done by a select few in a family. It's helping them balance what they know to be true with the way they feel. That's even more than valuable—it's invaluable.

The Bigger-Picture Perspective

I've mentioned this earlier, but can't reiterate enough how valuable your perspective on life can be to your children. How many of your kids have a trusted someone who is older, more experienced, wiser, or as available as you—especially someone within the context of family tradition, generational habits, and connected relationships? There aren't many. Besides, it's your job. Parents are the ones to bring hope to the table, looking beyond what is seen, and having faith because of their experiences in the past. Parents offer the bigger-picture perspective. That's invaluable.

Help with the Puzzle of Life

Ever put together one of those thousand-piece puzzles you spread out over a table and have your family gather around doing their part? It's funny to me that these usually take place at family events. The process pretty much reflects God's piecing together of His masterpiece through all the family members putting together their conglomeration of jagged parts.

Usually, people put together the borders first, kind of the outline of the work of art to come. The border holds the puzzle pieces together as they are joined and connected to create a beautiful picture. Everyone usually selects a part of the puzzle and begins their work. They search and try to make the pieces fit, just like in life. I don't know about you, but usually, during this table activity, I hear the following comments from my kids and grandkids:

- This piece doesn't fit.
- There are some pieces missing.
- I don't get how this is going to look.
- These just don't go together.

211

- I'm getting worn out.
- This is taking so much time.

Wise parents keep folks on course by responding with the following:

- This is how it fits together.
- Take your time; there's no hurry.
- Let's look at the bigger picture.
- Each piece is important.
- The dark pieces are just as needed as the brighter pieces.
- Keep going. It's coming together.

Throughout the process, wise parents explain how it takes all colors to bring about the majesty of this masterpiece (just like life). It takes time to get things right (just like life). The dark pieces make the brighter pieces come to life (just like life). See my point? Helping your kids put together a jigsaw puzzle is a lot like helping them put together the pieces of their lives. When you help them see and understand the similarities, that's invaluable. Wise parents sacrifice the important things of today for the more valuable stuff of the future. That's what they do best.

Wise parents sacrifice the important things of today for the more valuable stuff of the future.

CHAPTER 22

Won't Somebody Just Listen!

Do nothing out of selfish ambition or vain conceit. Rather, in humility value others above yourselves, not looking to your own interests but each of you to the interests of the others.

Philippians 2:3-4

If there is ever a time that adolescents are looking for someone to listen, it is now. Over the last few years, I've watched our culture move away from some very basic principles and values necessary for relational interaction, to an atmosphere where communication is more about the one-way expression of one's thoughts and beliefs, rather than the two-way street of someone actively listening to the heart of people struggling to be heard.

Throughout this book, I emphasize again and again how vital it is for parents to listen and actively show concern for the viewpoints of others. Effective communication and discussion depend on focusing on others more than yourself.

Let me use an example of a well-known group called Black Lives Matter, an organization formed in 2012. It is working to validate black lives. The slogan "Black Lives Matter" hit the news media a few years ago, and the immediate response was "All Lives Matter" from many across the country. This slogan became a springboard for other various slogans like "Blue Lives Matter," "Gay Lives Matter," and "Firefighters' Lives Matter." The focus of public response was shifted to other groups who tried to invalidate the Black Lives Matter message by stating that other lives matter just as much. In other words, people jumped to express their own beliefs, to override or ignore the initial message of Black Lives Matter.

Now, don't think this is a political statement. Please don't take my comments as a justification for anyone, and don't focus on the purpose and mission of any of these groups. I'm just pointing out the responses to this organization. I hardly know what any of the groups mentioned above believe or promote. It's just that I thought it odd that one group

Effective communication and discussion depend on focusing on others more than yourself.

wanted to be heard and shared their concern, and many chose to respond with their own favorite slogan rather than to listen. Many missed the original message the Black Lives Matter group was trying to communicate. In terms of true communication, the public's response was about as legitimate and effective as the following two examples.

My wife tearfully came to me years ago and in so many words said, "Mark, I was sexually abused for a number of years." If my response had been insensitive, "Well, Jan, there were a lot of people that were sexually abused," I'm sure it would have significantly affected our relationship and marriage. Her message would have been missed, her heart not heard because of my insensitivity and my need to respond rather than to listen.

What if my son came to me and shared that he was getting bullied at school and had been beaten up a few times, and my response was, "Well, a lot of people are bullied and beaten up at school?" I'm again sure this kind of response would shut down our relationship and probably preclude any future communication. If the request for help and reaching out for hope was ignored, then the heart would hardened by the hard-hearted response.

A young lady recently told me that she was conned by a young fellow and subsequently raped by him. She let me know that it was the first time that she was able to talk about the incident. She was vulnerable in her desire to share feelings and the heartache she had been carrying for a couple of years. Her words were shaky, her heart was pounding, and her chin quivered the whole time she poured out her heart. If I had even hinted with words that generalized her message, saying, "Well, honey, many young girls have been conned by young men and eventually raped," do you think that she would ever share anything with me again?

When people aren't heard, they start to scream the message louder. When that louder message isn't heard, then they become activists, actively behaving in a way to get other people's attention. Can you relate the same type of behavior to struggling teens?

I wonder if unruly children would have reached the point of acting out if their parents (or someone significant in their life) had actively listened. If parents can listen to the initial stages of their teen's problem, isn't it more likely to help their teen avoid getting hurt? I guarantee that a teen not paid attention to will eventually get attention one way or another.

The key to active listening is to understand what you hear. Be aware of your filters. Our filters interpret and translate how we hear the message coming from our children. Our filters might include how we were raised, our traditions, our hurts, our perceptions, our background, our own beliefs and our values. Our own trust issues, our age, and our experiences can taint the

Make it your goal to understand your children's world, and filter their message in the way that looks out for their interest, not your own.

messages we hear. The challenge is to remove our filters and listen through our children's grid. We need to understand where they are coming from, not filter what they're saying through where we've been. If we hear it how they're saying it, then we'll be connecting.

Make it your goal to understand your children's world, and filter their message in the way that looks out for their interest, not your own. Effective parents are good listeners who possess the ability to look to the interests of their teen's world and not lean on their own understanding of their own world. That's called participatory listening.

As I've said before, many parents get so intent on sharing their message that they forget about hearing the message from their teen. Your interaction with your child has got to be about them, not about you. A good listener has the ability to let people know they matter without saying a word. Good listeners have the amazing ability to speak to the heart because they understand where the heart of their child is.

Let me offer some practical ways to improve your listening skills with your children.

Invite Them Over

How you respond to your children early in life will determine how they respond to you later in life. Isn't it ironic how annoyed we can get when our younger kids always want something, ask for everything, and never quit talking? Then they enter their teen years, and we wish they would tell us what they want, ask us questions, and maintain discussions with us?

Let your teens know you are still there for them. The welcome mat is always out to discuss anything. Instead of always wanting to share your opinion, let them know you would love to hear what they have to say. When they speak, make sure you give them eye contact to let them know you are listening.

Listen Now, Don't Wait

Timing is everything. If the opportunity to listen arises, make it a priority. When teens want to talk, don't put them off or let it go until the weekend. If they have something on their hearts, then give them the opportunity to share it with you as soon as possible. Putting them off only sends the message that they just aren't important right now. If you find yourself always saying, "Let's talk later," you're missing some connecting opportunities.

Understand, Not Necessarily Agree

Chances are you are at least twenty-plus years older than your children. When they become teens, it means that you might try relating to them the way you remember the teen years…thirty-three years ago! That is a lot of years that have ushered in a world of change. So expect that there will be huge differences in the way your children perceive relationships and newsworthy events. Call it a generation gap, if you will. There are just differences—differences that will come up in your discussions.

Do this at the onset of a discussion: Let them know it is okay not to agree on everything. It's essential that the goal of your discussion be to bring you guys to an understanding, not necessarily agreement.

When teens want to have a discussion about a serious topic, whether it be abortion, marijuana, terrorism, war, or politics, I say this to them first. "I know that we won't agree on everything, but by helping me understand how you think, you may move me closer to appreciating your viewpoint." This comment diffuses any potential argument. Comments like this let your children know you don't want to argue. You want to discuss. Discussion stoppers and *fighting words* include, but are certainly not limited to, the following:

- Where did that come from?
- Who told you that?
- Are you kidding me?
- That's stupid.
- Did you come up with that on your own?

- That's hard to believe!
- That's wrong.

Some comments that help your conversation move forward positively are more along the lines of these:

- That's interesting.
- Wow, that's different.
- I never thought of that.
- Hmmmmm…
- I see where you're coming from.
- I've never heard it said that way before.

Hey, when I'm having a discussion with a teen, or any kid for that matter, I want to do all I can to ensure the conversation is engaging and will be one we can continue in the future. Don't you?

Don't Interrupt, It's a No-No

When you interrupt mid-sentence, interject a thought, or just blurt out what you're thinking and don't let your children complete their comments, you tell them you aren't listening. You're not valuing them. You're devaluing them. Let them finish their sentences and comments. Don't stop their flow of words. You've worked hard to get this fire going. Don't put it out with interruptions that douse any chance you'll have for further conversations.

If you're both interrupters, then set up a plan and say, "Hey, you speak a paragraph, and then let me speak a paragraph. I want to hear all you're saying and don't want to interrupt." One practical tool for interrupters is to pass an object back and forth. Give your children a penny, a rock, a dollar or whatever object you choose. Tell them you won't speak or respond to what they're saying until they pass you the chosen object. When you have the object, they can't speak. This can help you break the bad habit of interrupting.

Don't Correct During Conversations

Ever been in conversations where there's so much correction going on you forget what the subject of the conversation was in the first place? Correction quickly becomes a distraction from the conversation your child is trying to have with you. Conversational correction looks a lot like this:

Son:	Mom, we spent two hours at the swimming pool.
Mom:	No, it was one-and-a-half hours.
Son:	Okay. And I swam six laps on my own.
Mom:	No, it was only four.
Son:	Okay. Then we left to get a hamburger.
Mom:	No, you had a cheeseburger.
Son:	Okay, we came home, and I took a nap for an hour.
Mom:	No, it was thirty minutes.
Son:	Whatever….just forget it.

You get the picture from this conversation. What is it about people that they can't leave well enough alone and just let someone have a conversation without correcting any possible misinformation? What happens in these situations is that eventually the child will have a conversation only in the presence of one, avoiding the corrector's presence. Most teens would rather not share anything than have a discussion full of correction.

Bring Value to the Conversation

Parents may have jobs where people listen, value their opinions, and can't wait to hear what they have to say. But they come home, and no one wants to listen to what they have to say. They may feel like they've lost their value. They no longer contribute. They miss the position of prestige they hold with others at their workplace. Basically, they get pretty used to the praise and value they receive from the interactions they have with people outside the home, and they kind of hope the same will happen in their home.

If you miss the validation you get from your job and at your workplace, you may try to recoup it in your conversations with those around you now (usually your spouse and kids). Ask yourself how much of your conversation is an attempt to get value from the person you're communicating with rather than bringing value to them.

If this applies to you, I want you to know you don't have to prove your value. You are exempt from having to do so because you are a parent. You don't have to prove anything to anyone. You are already valued because of who you are. Your kids show you the value you hold by merely coming to you for wisdom, to ask questions, or to sit in your presence and hear your stories. You are more than important, more than valuable. You are invaluable.

Focus on Your Children

You've had a lifetime of people listening to you. It's your turn to listen to your children. I love this paraphrasing of Scripture that I mentioned earlier.

Spouting off before listening to the facts is both shameful and foolish. (Proverbs 18:13, NLT)

Let me ask you one more time. Do you listen, or do you just wait to talk? Foolish parents hear something and, instead of trying to truly listen, respond quickly because they know the answer and want to be the first to hit the buzzer with the right answer. It's like they're on a game show competing with others. They have to win, and they have to be right. Many parents are

Many parents are more concerned with what their response will be than about hearing their children's heart behind their questions.

more concerned with what their response will be than about hearing their children's heart behind their questions. They want to make sure they sound good rather than listening and interpreting well. They might be more intent on sharing their story than listening to that of their teens. The best parents remember that they've had a lifetime to be heard, now it's their teen's turn.

Repeat Back What They Just Said

Remember the age difference between you and your kids, which I mentioned about earlier? If you're striving to understand what they are saying, but you're not sure you get it, repeat what you hear back to them.

"Okay, this is what I'm hearing you say. Am I getting it right?"
"Is this what I'm hearing you communicate?"

It's an easy way to keep the discussion on track. It helps prevent you from wandering down conversational bunny trails. It ensures that you're picking up on the heart of what they want to say; while helping them put their feelings into words, which they might not even know how to say. Teens are dying for someone to listen and hear.

I know a young man named Mike who struggled at home. He often said to me that he had a tough time finding someone who would just listen to him. Mike was not a bad kid. He just wanted to have a relationship with someone who would show a bit of compassion and empathy as he wrestled with normal adolescent issues.

He was one of those kids that thought a little more deeply than most teens. As a result, he felt things a little more deeply as well. Mike struggled with a little bit of depression. He rejected my suggestion of going to see a counselor so he would have someone to talk to. "They're always trying to fix me instead of listening to what I have to say," Mike said. He just wanted to be heard.

In desperation, this young man got to the end of his rope, figuratively and literally. He tried to hang himself. Finally, that got the attention of those around him. He didn't die, but he did damage his spine to the point that he'll spend the rest of his life in a wheelchair. Mike told me that his unsuccessful attempt to kill himself was so that the people he loved would read the six-page letter he wrote describing what he was feeling and thinking all along. All Mike wanted was someone to listen. It almost cost his life.

Teens are dying for someone just to listen. Don't pay that awful price. Be the listening ear they need.

The fool speaks, the wise man listens.
—Ethiopian proverb

CHAPTER 23

Play it Smart; They're Watching

Let us not love with words or speech but with actions and in truth.

1 John 3:18

Actions speak louder than words."

"It's not what you say; it's what you do."

"I can't hear what you're saying because your actions are speaking too loud."

You've heard these sayings before, I know. You can't live as long as we all have without finding some placard or post that encourages integrity and promotes truthfulness. Your kids will know you by what you do, not what you say you will do. The question to answer would be, "Do the words out of my mouth match the actions my kids see in my life?" When words and actions line up, that's called integrity. The character traits of honesty, fairness, truthfulness, sincerity, and trustworthiness will be validated or invalidated by the actions they see. Be careful; they're watching.

In your children's earlier years, they accept anything and everything you say. When they get into their teen years, observation becomes more important. They are beginning to understand that they live in a culture which offers them fake news, fake social structures, fake friends, and fake media. Remember what I mentioned before? Appearance and performance matter more than honesty and honor. Kids don't innately know the difference between counterfeit and real. They learn the difference from trial and error in their earlier adolescent years. This sets them on a course to seek out those relationships that are genuine and authentic. It is my hope that they find someone genuine and authentic in you. Be a trustworthy parent who can be relied upon to be true to your word and deeds.

> When words and actions line up, that's called integrity.

Here is what I think integrity looks like for parents. There is a *vulnerability* that shows who you really are, coupled with a willingness to express emotion and identify your own hurt and struggles. I used to think the honor given to parents came because of their ability to hide their character flaws and escape observation by only visiting for short lengths of time. I thought parents smiled, doled out hugs, and never revealed their true selves. I now think otherwise.

Teens are intrinsically good at sniffing out fakes. They know when they're having the wool pulled over their eyes. Removing yourself from observation isn't the answer. Exposure of your true self is. The more they know about who you are, flaws and all, the closer the relationship will be. Vulnerability entails being open about who you are. You admit struggles, confess failures, and disclose past mistakes. These confessions make you more human. If parents failed and still came out okay, then children can fail and know they'll make it through.

I've met parents and grandparents who never wanted anyone to know they were married before. Many never let anyone know they had an abortion, smoked pot during college, or got fired from a job. Others hesitate to admit any failure, mistake, blunder, time spent in jail, or illegal activities. Lots of parents are cautious to admit past wrongdoing, never realizing that admission and confession clear the path for open and frank relationships. Some are never open about anything, and the mysteries of their lives are taken to their graves. When all faults remain hidden and pushed under the carpet, genuineness and authenticity never happen in a relationship.

Confidence would be another trait of integrity. When parents are confident, that confidence can be transferred to their children. It's about being comfortable in your own skin, not fearful of someone seeing the real deal. Vulnerability is about being open; confidence is an assuredness of who you are and whose you are.

The trait of *honesty* can be seen when parents answer questions or when they ask someone else a question. People who are honest speak the truth in love, aren't going to let wrongdoings slide, and call a spade a spade without beating around the bush. Honesty can be seen when a mother admits and apologizes for the times she has gossiped or nagged. Honesty can be seen in a father who admits the truth when asked by a son if he has ever had a problem with pornography. Honest people return what isn't theirs, answer questions truthfully, and never hide things. Honesty is the truth, the whole truth, and nothing but the truth.

Honest parents come clean before it's too late. If there's been a *chink in the armor*, it's repaired so their message and legacy remain intact. The hope they've transferred to their kids rings true long after they're gone.

Responsibility for one's actions, past and present, is so important in the development of a healthy young adult. Good parents make sure they model responsibility, especially because their children, and others, are watching them. Moms and dads who model responsibility show their loved ones they never have to worry about cleaning up any messes left behind when they die. There is no unfinished business others have to take care of.

Responsibility means taking your skeletons out of the closet, accepting responsibility for them being there in the first place, and being vulnerable and honest enough to lay claim to what you have done. All this gives you the opportunity to share your story of your redemption.

Those who are full of integrity are *secure* enough to speak their mind and stand up for what is right and true. These folks confront wrongdoing and don't tolerate the violation of their core principles. They trust in themselves and their belief system and don't waste time worrying about what others think. They are not swayed but remain steady. They know God is in control, so they don't have to be.

Another aspect of integrity is a *willingness to take risks*, not be afraid of failure. I'm not talking about financial investments or jumping out of an airplane. I'm talking about taking risks in relationships, confronting what is wrong, speaking the truth in love, exposing your past, risking your reputation for a deeper relationship, and taking responsibility for wrongdoing when it may mean some type of consequence.

Parents with integrity *practice what they preach.*

And lastly, parents with integrity *practice what they preach*. Period. They are the opposite of hypocrites or being two-faced. They eliminate falseness and double standards. They approach life with sincerity. Their words and actions never contradict themselves.

How do you rate? Are you a dad or a mom with integrity? Wherever you land on the scale, all the integrity in the world won't impact your kids unless you are involved in their lives and give them the opportunity to see you for who you are. Be around. Be steady. Be vulnerable. Be honest. Be responsible. If you want your children to become men and women with integrity, you have to model it first. Your family's legacy largely depends on you.

Integrity takes consistency. You can't be one kind of person in front of the kids and another kind of person when they're not around. Your reputation will precede you. Double standards don't fly.

Here's a personal story. I travel a lot. I'm on and off planes every week speaking somewhere around the country. As a result, I've learned to travel well by myself and am pretty self-sufficient when it comes to planes, trains, and automobiles (and hotels). I can get where I need to go pretty easily and return home without any anxiety or strife because I've learned how to make it all work.

When I travel with others, I'm easily frustrated. They don't travel like I do. They obviously don't understand how this traveling thing works. They don't want to eat where I want to eat, don't follow my time schedule and my way of operating. How rude! Okay, in other words, I'm pretty self-centered when I travel.

I can ruin a vacation before we even get there, yet when I arrive at our destination, I can have a blast and enjoy the time with everyone. I'm not sure they enjoy the time with me because of the way I acted in the process of getting to our destination. It's not where you vacation but how you get there that counts.

I need to be a man of integrity when I travel solo, and the same man of integrity when I travel with others, especially my family. I have to remind myself that how we get there is more important than the vacation itself, in terms of how they perceive me and accept my role in their lives.

I want those around me not to wait to say great things about me until after I'm gone to my final destination. I want them to enjoy my presence as we travel together through this thing called life. The more genuine and authentic I am can make all the difference in how we travel together. Your kids need you to be their model of genuineness and authenticity. They need you, and they're watching your every move.

CHAPTER  24

A Legacy of Relationship

Therefore I intend always to remind you of these qualities, though you know them and are established in the truth that you have.

2 Peter 1:12 (ESV)

I can promise you these three things: You're going to die sometime after you read this book. It's going to happen sooner than you think. It's not going to happen the way you want it to happen.

There's something about embracing the inevitability of life ending one day that has a way of focusing you on what is most important today. It helps you live smarter and look at each day as a blessing. Yesterday, I went to a restaurant and the waitress asked me, "Are you celebrating anything today?" "Yes, I am," I said. "I woke up this morning, and that's worth celebrating."

If you're feeling that brisk fall wind of change, ushering in a transition of the seasons in your life, then no doubt you are also wondering a bit about what your life has been about. You start to focus on what will be remembered about you once you are gone. Some folks don't care, and when they are gone, they will quickly be forgotten, except for an occasional search on Ancestry.com or when some relative is flipping through old family photos.

Then there are those of us who want to pass something on. We want to know our lives meant something more than mere existence. We want to see how we impacted someone else. We want to make others' lives better and our time on Earth significant. We want to know we made a difference.

I'm not sure I thought about this when my own kids were born. Jan and I were so ecstatic about having kids (and scared to death), that we only thought about how we were going to survive. We were both twenty-one years old, managing apartments, going to school full-time, and working two jobs while leading a Young Life club for kids. When Melissa and Adam were born, we saw a miracle happen before our eyes. We never regretted having kids early, but we weren't focusing on our legacy back then.

When our grandkids were born, we encountered new feelings of getting older, wanting to make an impact, and thinking about life from a different perspective. Our kids changed the way we lived; our grandkids changed our hearts and our focus.

There was something so different about having grandkids that my whole perspective on life changed. It was no longer about making money, doing a great job, building a career, and involving myself in everything good I could find. It was more about impact, knowing these little kids that I was holding, who would eventually call me Poppa, are the ones who would carry on any family legacy, if there was going to be one. They were the hope for future generations of our family. It was then that I asked myself, *what do you want to be known for?*

Short of making the history books, setting records, or committing some heinous crime, most of us will be forgotten when our grandkids are gone. Our work may be remembered, something we wrote or videotaped may be read or viewed, but our legacy will only extend as far as our relationships with our grandkids.

Your legacy will be written in two places. One is on your tombstone. Now, I don't know about you, but I don't know many people who run around cemeteries with the intent of gathering wisdom from the one-liners on tombstones. This headstone monument thing seems a bit overrated to me. People always ask me what I want written as my epitaph, like there's going to be thousands of people visiting my buried carcass to see what my life was about. I really don't care what's on my marker. I'm sure it will say when I was born and when I died, like all the neighbors planted in my new neighborhood.

Okay, I'm digressing a bit here, but after a funeral, when do you ever see a person's headstone again? When you're laying another family member to rest, but that's really not the best time to be searching for some tombstone wisdom. So I don't think too much about what will be chiseled about me after I'm gone.

The second place your legacy will be written is in the hearts of those who know you. In particular, those you have known. A legacy is not about depositing a few gold nuggets of wisdom that will be remembered by all. You're not a box of fortune cookies—clever but not very deep. A legacy is not just doing a whole lot of good for others. A real legacy is the connection you made with family through the deep relationships you had with them. A legacy is found within the hope and wisdom you've passed down to your children and grandchildren, the truths they can pass down to the next generation. Parents who leave a legacy are not only remembered for what they contributed, but also for the life-giving qualities they provided to those around them.

A real legacy is the connection you made with family through the deep relationships you had with them.

My main concern is not everyone out there. My main concern is the health and welfare of my own family. That's where I want to make the most difference, in the lives of my wife, my kids (including my son- and daughters-in-law, even though I can't tell the difference between them because I consider them all the same), and my grandkids.

I've been to many funerals, and it's interesting to see who attends.

When my mom died, the people who attended were a few of her friends, a couple from her Sunday school, a couple of neighbors, and a few folks from some of the organizations where she volunteered. The remaining people attending was our whole family. The attendance at a funeral speaks loudly to the legacy that deceased person left for their family. All the wisdom shared through your legacy, should it go any further than your life, will go as far as your grandkids or great-grandkids. That's good enough for me.

I'll leave it to the next generation to take care of their grandkids; I'm just trying to keep up with the four I have. My point in all this is to ask you, "What do you want to be known for?" My real hope is you'll ask that question for yourself. Then answer it and live the answer.

I think about that when I'm introduced to people, run into acquaintances, and when someone introduces me to an audience before I speak. I've been described to crowds and individuals in so many ways that many times I chuckle and think, "Is this really how they see me?" At least a few times I've cocked my head and asked, "Is this really what I want to be known for?"

I was recently at a Texas Rangers baseball game and ran into a fellow named Aaron Watson. He's a country music artist and a great fellow. He introduced me to his wife as, "Honey, this is the guy that sends us that pecan pie for Christmas every year." Many people just know me as "Jan's husband." Others introduce me as, "This is Mark, and he's the guy that lives with all those kids in East Texas." Some remember me as, "That guy with the mustache." Many of our Heartlight parents introduce me to their friends as, "He's the one I was telling you about that cooks those great steaks." When speaking at seminars or conferences, I'm known as "That guy on the radio."

A few weeks ago, Amy Grant introduced me to her husband, Vince Gill. I was excited to finally meet him. Amy and Vince are warm, genuinely kind people. No joke, her introduction was, "Vince, this is the guy who lives with those struggling teens and has all those cabins that are joined by walkways." I'm not kidding.

I can see it on my tombstone now: "Here lies Mark, the pie guy on the radio who has a mustache and lives with all those kids, who is married to Jan and cooks a great steak and has cabins all joined by walkways." Not exactly what I was going for in my legacy. Not quite what I want to be known for. I know this: Legacy is all about relationships. Not just my relationship with my grandkids, but my grandkids' relationships with me. I want to know them, and I want to be known by them.

Your relationship with your kids can be the most important relationship they have during their teen years.

I recently heard a young lady who stated simply, "Stop trying to be there for me when you know nothing about me." It reminded me that having an impact on someone doesn't just happen because we know them or when we do something that can benefit their life. It's all about relationship, about getting to know them and know them well. It's communicating life across a bridge of relationship, which doesn't stop if they don't respond. It's offering your life to them regardless of what comes back to you.

Family relationships are tricky. I've heard many families tell me they can all get along if they don't talk about religion or politics. Others tell me that as long as they don't bring up other certain topics, then the holidays will go well. I've always thought relationships have to be more than that. Relationships, true relationships, don't need to be bound by restrictions but rather be freed up to flourish.

If you're going to have freedom within your relationships, then you might have to accept the fact that it's okay to disagree. At times you may be polar opposites, but your relationship can still thrive.

Your relationship with your kids can be the most important relationship they have during their teen years. Don't mess it up by requiring your kids to believe, act, and present themselves the way you do. The relationship is always the most important thing, because if you don't have a relationship, then you will never be able to have those much-needed discussions that may bring about a different way of thinking. You'll never have talks to disperse the wisdom you have accumulated. You'll eliminate the chance to have influence and opportunity to shape their thinking and mold their values.

Parents, even if you don't accept the lifestyle and choices your children make, don't *throw the baby out with the bath water*. If you do, you won't have a chance to touch the hearts of those who long for your presence in their lives.

Legacies don't just happen.
They're made.

I meet kids all the time who are involved in activities I don't approve of. I hear teens spouting off comments and beliefs I'll never embrace. I see people living lifestyles I don't agree with. I meet with girls who are making stupid decisions with their bodies, who are engaged in activities that are immoral at best and destructive at worst. I see young men making poor choices and countering anything that resembles biblical standards and moral principles.

I can reject them and their lifestyles and never have an influence, or I can love them right where they are and hope to steer them in another direction. I'll say it one more time. Accepting them does not mean that I accept their choices, lifestyle, behaviors, or actions. I'm not condoning when I don't correct. I can love them in spite of their behaviors. I know actions are an expression of their hearts, and that's what I want to influence.

Relationship matters.

Regardless of the differences of opinions or the inconsistencies in your beliefs, the relationships with your children matter. You can have an amazing impact on the lives of your kids, even when your beliefs are miles apart. You are the one who can offer the hope and help they are desperately looking for. You have the ability to leave a legacy no one else can. Leave a good one, filled with family members who remember in detail the positive impact your life had on them. It's a pay-it-forward kind of thing. Just as others had an impact on you and changed your life, I'm sure you have a desire to have an impact on others.

Legacies don't just happen. They're made. Keep making yours today. If you haven't started yet, there's no time to waste.

CHAPTER 25

When Your Teen is Struggling

Like one who takes away a garment on a cold day, or like vinegar poured on a wound, is one who sings songs to a heavy heart.

Proverbs 25:20

Giving your teen control of his or her life is easy when all is going well, and there haven't been too many "bumps in the road" that have challenged you or caused a crisis within your family. But it's a lot harder when your teen seems to be spinning "out of control." So, let's spend some time discussing what to look for and how to put together a comprehensive plan to stop the negative and inappropriate behavior, and continue to help your child assume responsibility for his or her life.

When all isn't working as planned, everything looks a little different. Perhaps you've been reading this book and are ready to explode because we're not dealing with everything that seems to be falling apart. Or maybe you've tried all I'm suggesting and it's just not working. As a matter of fact, it's still a mess. It's hard to talk about helping a child make good decisions when all your teen is doing is screwing up and making poor choices. It's hard to hear about success when you feel like a failure, and harder to get excited over purchasing a lake house when you're drowning in a lake. A child spinning out of control isn't a single and isolated event. It consumes you and affects everything around you.

Here's an example:

We lost a home in a tornado in Tulsa, Oklahoma, many years ago. But it wasn't just the twister that caused the chaos and crisis. It was the rain that flooded everything. It was the lack of electricity that kept the darkness present, as we fumbled to gain our footing. It was the smell of leaking gas, looters, and collateral damage of pets killed, people injured, and debris everywhere, which only complicated the mess that this swirling storm had caused. Communication was down. We felt alone, and we felt we had lost everything. Emotions were high, comfort was low, and the feeling of loss was overwhelming.

This sounds like a family in crisis, a severe disaster. If you've been there, you know exactly what I mean. It's when you find out that your daughter is having sex with her new boyfriend, and she has become disrespectful, sneaky, damaging, and lost. It's when your son is angry and takes it out on you. He's failing school because he can't (or won't) get out of bed. You've found drugs or paraphernalia in his room, and the once lovable young man is now a torment in your home. Maybe there's been a suicide attempt or a divorce, which has divided your family, or a tragedy that a child just can't get over. It's in these times that I tell parents, lean not on your own understanding, but get help, and get it fast!

Here are some warning signs that might alert you to an oncoming storm:

1. Your teen becomes verbally irritable and openly expressive.
2. Grades are slipping, if they haven't already fallen.
3. Depression is setting in, and sleep patterns have dramatically changed.

4. Old friends are gone, and new friends of a different sort are present.

5. What they once loved, they now hate; what they once hated, they now love.

6. They withdraw socially.

7. Sexual activity is on the rise.

8. Defiance is present, and totally ignoring you is rampant.

9. Extreme weight loss or weight gain.

10. Cutting marks can be seen on their arms.

11. Anxiety overload is moving to a complete shutdown.

12. A "disconnect" is happening in all relationships.

If you see any of these things happening, it's time for a change, before it gets any worse. If you feel that, at any time, your child's life is in danger, you must act today. If it is a slow-moving disintegration, then ask yourself a question. If your teen continues on the same path, where will he or she be in six months? If your teen is not in a better place, action must be taken to find a safe haven for your child. Engage people that can handle situations when your attempts to do so are failing.

You must approach the change you see happening in your teen with three different components working together. All three of these areas are essential to the overall health of your family.

1. Relational

I've mentioned this earlier. The relationship you have with your children is important, if not the most important relationship they have. I say this regardless of what message they are communicating to you. If you're not there to speak truth into their lives in their darkest moment, who will be?

I encourage parents to adopt three different focal points of discipline. They are what I call the "3 Ds": Dishonesty, Disrespect, and Disobedience.

The common thread through these three intentional behaviors is that each, if allowed to continue, are relationship destroyers and not just with family members. It's with everyone. So, what you teach your teens about these 3 Ds will affect them the rest of their lives.

The bottom line is: Relationships are important, and that must be the foremost purpose of dealing with inappropriate behavior. Let your teens know that you will not allow them to destroy their relationship with you or with those around them. And keep moving toward them if they try to do so.

> Relationships are important, and that must be the foremost purpose of dealing with inappropriate behavior.

Let them know that there is nothing they can do to keep you from moving toward them relationally. So many times, the behavior you see is really just a scream for help or a ploy for attention, which is so desperately needed. Words of affirmation are needed, comments of encouragement are necessary, and time spent together is crucial.

Spend a lot of time trying to figure out what it is about your relationship with your teen that is keeping you all from progressing. As stated earlier, teens change because of relationship. That's why it's important that you keep the one you have with your teen.

2. Structure of Your Home

Develop rules and consequences that are specific, definite, and understandable, stating what you want from them and what you'll do for them. Reward those behaviors that you want to see, and establish consequences for behaviors that you don't want to see. Make it a package deal by saying, "I'm asking these things *from you*: no drugs, be respectful, meet with a counselor, take your meds. And I'm willing to do these things *for you*: I'll ease up on some rules, give you more control, and help you with finances."

Somebody might say, Mark! That's manipulation! You're darn right it is. When you have a child that is spinning out of control, you'll do anything to keep them from spiraling down a path that will damage them for the rest of their life.

Develop rules and consequences that are specific, definite, and understandable, stating what you want from your teen.

Develop rules and set the consequences. You don't really need a whole lot of rules—just the five main rules that if followed, would change the destiny of your family. Be willing to lose a few battles along the way to ensure that you will win the war. Figure out which "hill to die on" and determine those potential conflicts that will soon pass on their own.

3. Dealing with Issues Behind the Behavior

Remember earlier when I stated that something is going on behind the behavior you see? There may be some unknown medical issue. Your child may have some deep-seated thinking processes that require the help of a professional. Your teen might need medical intervention or need to take meds to help control some behaviors that just won't be regulated in another way. Your child might need a counselor to meet with regularly. You might want to get a psychiatrist or psychologist to perform a psychological assessment to see if your teen is just "wired" differently. Hospitalization may be needed if your child becomes a danger to himself or herself.

You can make progress in every area of your home, but if you don't deal with the core issue "pushing" your teen's behavior, you'll have a difficult time moving ahead in your relationship with your teen. You might have some great rules and boundaries established in your home, have a great relationship, and yet not deal with the real issues behind the behavior. You'll find that changes you see will be temporary with no long-lasting change. Or you can deal with the issues behind the behavior and have the structure all lined out, but with no relationship, your teen will continue to fall apart. You need everything working together.

You must deal with all three areas, and balance your focus on each, to effectively get your child back into control of his or her life, and bring sanity back into your home.

To those of you who are reading this and feel that deep, dark struggle with your teen happening right now, I would encourage you to talk to someone. Meet with a counselor who can help you understand that you're not crazy. Talk with other parents who have similar issues, as it will help you understand that you are not alone. And take a break from the craziness of dealing with an out-of-control teen.

I'm amazed at the amount of stress a struggling teen can place on a marriage and other siblings within the family. Your family is no exception. This is where I would encourage you to lean not on your own understanding, but reach out, let your struggle be known, and allow others to surround you with their love, support, and help.

No book written will solve a major crisis with your child. I would be foolish to think that reading a paragraph in thirty minutes will solve a situation that may have been brewing for years. While most of the things I've spoken about in this book can help, don't let the regional crisis of one teen spread to an all-out war for the whole family. Get help early, and get it from sources you can trust.

And I want you to know this:

1. This struggle is temporary. Second Corinthians 4:17 states, *"For our light and momentary struggles..."* It's a bump in the road, which will end soon...hopefully, before your teen heads off to college, gets a job, gets married, or goes into the military.

2. Conflict is a precursor to change. Conflict ushers in the opportunity for something different.

WHEN YOUR TEEN IS STRUGGLING

3. God will finish what He has started. Philippians 1:6 says, *"He who began a good work in you will carry it on to completion."*

4. Galatians 6:9 says, *"Let us not become weary in doing good, for at the proper time we will reap a harvest if we do not give up."*

Hang in there, my friend. No situation is hopeless.

CHAPTER 26

Making Memories Before
You Lose Yours

*And I will make every effort to see that after my departure you
will always be able to remember these things.*

2 Peter 1:15

The question that looms for many parents in their time of reflection is, "What do I want to be known for?" Maybe the more important question is, "How will they remember me?" It's not necessarily what you want to be known for that counts, but how they will recount their times with you.

It's been said that the moods of a lifetime can be found in the all-but-forgotten experiences of adolescence. That doesn't mean that a vacation or trip together before adolescence is nonexistent in the memories of your children. It just means those remembered the most clearly and enjoyed the most will be the ones taken between the ages of twelve to twenty.

One of my greatest fears is that when I die, the money I saved and invested gets distributed to my family, and I don't get to spend it on creating experiences while I am with them. I don't want to miss these moments because I am too darn busy. Money sure hasn't been my focus, but I saved diligently so Jan and I would be taken care of in our later years. Now, I'm more concerned with the memories in my family's hearts than I am about the amount of money in my bank account.

I was recently reminded of the futility of gathering and collecting everything we do in life, knowing that none of it can be taken with us when we die. I attended the funeral of my dear friend David Muth (who I mentioned

It's not necessarily what you want to be known for that counts, but how your teens will recount their times with you.

earlier) after he succumbed to his fight with Parkinson's. I arrived in Indiana for his funeral and walked in after the service began. I was ushered to the front to sit with his wife and daughters. I sat through the service holding the hands of his girls and looking at him in the casket. As I walked up to see my friend, I noticed that his wife, Amy, had put memorabilia of sorts in the casket propped up around David—pictures of times together, items that stirred memories with this wonderful man, and a few trinkets that meant nothing to most, yet were invaluable to the family. It was touching, to say the least, and my eyes kept dripping on the casket as I recalled the wonderful times we had together.

What was not there in the casket was money. No cash, no checkbook, nor were there any pictures of dollar bills. No car, no valuable possessions were being buried with him. When we loaded him up for the graveside, there was no U-Haul attached to his hearse. Just him and the beautiful memories he created for his family.

If you can't take any of it with you, then spend it on experiences that last a lifetime and leave a legacy. Spend times together that bind the hearts in relationship together. This crazy disease took away David's time here on Earth, but it couldn't take away his family's beautiful memories of their times together. Though painful to remember, those memories are, and always will be, wonderfully inscribed in the hearts of those he loved. Money is a great inheritance. It's a bonus, a gift, a blessing from left field, usually not anticipated and always greatly appreciated. However, why wait until you're gone to share a little of it?

I was reminded of how a little went a long way when I gave my granddaughter twenty dollars to support a car wash that she was participating in. She was so grateful and excited that I helped. A simple twenty-dollar bill...that's all it took to let her know I cared about what she cared about. For me, it was a reminder to her that when she needs something, I want her to come to me to ask. That doesn't keep her from going to her own parents or others she knows, but it affirms our relationship in a way that will keep her coming back for more than just money.

One of these days, I'm going to write checks for ten thousand dollars and give one to each of my grandkids. It's one of my goals. It is founded on a wish I had that was never fulfilled. When Jan and I were first married, we had no money. We struggled to make ends meet. It was a great date night if we were able to air-pop some popcorn and sit and watch a movie. I painted apartments in the evening, cleaned toilets, unclogged drains, worked two jobs, and was ecstatic when Young Life decided to pay me twenty-five dollars a month as I volunteered.

At one point, I remember we had a health insurance payment due of twenty-two dollars. I took my high school ring to a pawnshop and got twenty-three dollars for it. I paid the bill and ended up with one dollar in my pocket. I remember thinking, *I just wish someone would help us in some way.* We had a baby due, I was a student at Tulsa University, and Jan dropped out of nursing school because of morning sickness.

That's when I said to myself, *one of these days, I'm going to give some money to my grandkids at just the right time.* Now I'm thinking, *Why not?* I might as well give it to them while I'm alive and enjoy their excitement and pleasure than wait until I'm gone and everything is divvied up among my heirs anyway. Here's the only catch I'll put with the money. Each of my grandkids will be charged with giving the same amount to their own grandchildren one day when those grandkids need it the most. It's kind of a pay-it-forward deal, the start of a new tradition for our family.

Chances are, by the time my kids get my inheritance, they really won't need it. They'll be making their own living and making ends meet. But unexpected windfalls give you the chance to do things, go places, or experience something you might not budget for otherwise. If I can give them that joy, why not give it now?

The inheritance you leave is about more than dollars; it's about leaving an impact on your kids and grandkids. Events and occasions that trigger memories are important. These open the door to the life skills you shared, the legacy you've built in their lives, and reminds them of the special relationship you had with them.

When your children remember you, what will they remember you for?

The experiences with you are important. They open the doors to the hearts of your children. My family has wonderful memories of going to the beach. After I'm buried or burnt, I hope that every time my family is at the beach, they'll remember my love for the ocean, the wind, the waves, and the sea life we all enjoyed watching together. Those are great memories, but I want them to recall more than just, *hey, remember how Poppa loved the beach?*

My wife Jan has populated East Texas with birds, as she feeds them every day. We have every type of bird you can imagine darting in and out of our backyard on a daily basis. Friends give her bird towels, bird glasses, bird gifts, and bird emblems. She's known as the bird lady. If that's all she's known as, that's kind of weird. If people think of Jan when they see a bird and remember nothing else about her, then her legacy will pass quickly and soon be forgotten.

But I think Jan is creating much more of a legacy. I think when friends and loved ones see birds, they will think of Jan. When they think of her and the memories they have of her, they'll also remember her love of animals, her ability to talk to anyone, her fun-loving personality, her strength through pain, her ability to listen well, her efforts to make everyone's life better, the lessons she taught, her love for God, and her ability to share how she found so much in Him. They'll think about how she laughed in the face of conflict, how she gave generously, and how her words were full of wisdom. They'll remember all of these things because even a bunch of feathery friends stir memories of

The inheritance you leave is about more than dollars; it's about leaving an impact on your kids and grandkids.

deeper connections of who she really was to others. Do you have memories built up in the hearts of your kids that will remind them of you? It's never too late to start.

Twenty years ago, I had this crazy idea to pile up all the Christmas trees from all the houses at Heartlight and burn them on New Year's Eve. The next year we stuffed some fireworks in the trees. The following year we added gasoline. Every year, the blaze gets bigger and bigger. This family tradition has now turned into a community event. People come from everywhere to see the Christmas tree burning at the Gregston's place. It's a memory that will be with our family for years. Now, I'm not suggesting you do the same. I don't know where you live, and you might get in trouble doing something in the city we habitually do in the country. I do suggest you create something memorable, magnificent, and meaningful to your family.

Think about what smells remind your kids of you? Is it that special candle you always burn, the perfume or cologne you wear, or the smell of your cooking at various times of the year? Whenever I smell boiling shrimp, I think of my dad. Is there a smell that is just unique to your home that reminds them of you? We had a young lady at Heartlight a couple of years ago that made a statement reflecting on her memory of home. She said she would occasionally go into her closet and open up her suitcase so she could *get a whiff of home.* The scent reminded her of what she missed dearly.

Start some traditions around your home. Perhaps it is leaving a jigsaw puzzle on the dining room table for everyone to gather and piece together. Maybe it's nights around the fireplace where everyone just catches up. Have you thought of having a joke night around the dinner table every Saturday night? Popping a champagne bottle on New Year's Eve? Or eating a special cultural meal to remind you of your heritage?

What is unique about you that you could teach your son or daughter? Do you play a musical instrument? If so, purchase one for your children and help them learn. Teach them how to do carpentry, operate a tractor, use some tools, build something, repair fence line, or care for and feed some animals. (Can you tell we live in the country?) Find one of your skills and talents and teach it to another.

Find a lifelong sport or activity you can do with your children. I'm talking about golf, tennis, horseback riding, weight lifting or working out, shooting guns at a gun range, hunting, or any activity that can be done throughout the rest of your kids' lives. Schedule a time to go on a mission trip with your children or volunteer somewhere local on a regular basis together. Go somewhere they'll go with no one else and keep a laid-back schedule that isn't filled with constant activity, so you have plenty of time for personal interaction.

Take a vacation and invite the whole family. When you go, eat a special meal that second night (after all have rested up) and share with them the beauty of family and how you want this trip to be an annual event.

Take a daughter to an event that wows them, a concert by a favorite artist, a backstage experience, a Broadway musical, or a big sports event. My granddaughter Maile and I have gone to the Country Music Awards each year for eight years now. We even attended the CMA Festival in Nashville this year, and I let her bring a couple of her friends. It will be an annual event for us as long as she wants to go and I am able. I really can't afford to do that, but I can't afford *not* to. Where would your daughter or son love to go? Why not make plans to take them?

What do you do on special holidays? Is there a ritual around your home? Is there a tradition to eat a Thanksgiving meal and then watch football or soccer all afternoon? Do you go to a Christmas Eve service, come home and open presents, and then spend Christmas afternoon going to a newly released movie?

As they get older, plan on some time where all can sit around and talk—not just be entertained. Go horseback riding, take a walk on the beach, ride ATV's around somewhere, shoot skeet in someone's field, or go to the symphony or a play and then out to eat.

Plan a fishing or hunting trip of a lifetime or a shopping spree in a place your kids have never been. Go to a tropical island or take that trip to Disney World, which you've always wanted to take. If you can't go, send others so they can have a wonderful experience.

Do something special on birthdays, the beginning of school, graduations, and weddings. Make it special by your attendance, but also provide something for those events that makes them—and your participation in them—memorable.

Spend time around a fireplace or an open fire on a cold night, whether it is in your backyard, on a beach, or on a mountaintop. Make it special.

If you have grandkids, have a week where you entertain them when they come to visit you. Make those memories by cooking great meals and letting them wear you out. When you can no longer do that at your home, go someplace else to make it happen.

These are all memory makers that will bring you to mind. When you're gone and there is a trigger that reminds them of you, it will prompt them to recall the loving impact you had on their life.

Personally, I love the idea and thought that my kids will remember me every time they smell the burning of powder and see the beauty of rockets, explosives, and fireworks. I'm sure those will bring a smile to their faces as they remember all the times we burnt up some Christmas trees and ushered in the New Year.

But that's not the only thing I want them to remember about me. I want that memory and other memories of me to remind them of the wisdom I shared along the way. I want them to recall, and put to good use in their lives, the particular and specific nuggets of truth demonstrated by the way I treated them and the way they saw me treat other people.

Make some memories before you lose yours. The remembrance of your generosity and kindness will last many lifetimes. Yes, memories of you will last. Make sure they are good ones. This is the time of life to make sure all unfinished business gets taken care of. Is there something hidden in your closet? Are there skeletons that might come out after you pass away that could taint the memories of your good times together with your family? Is anything currently unresolved between you and any family member? Come clean and take care of the business of forgiveness and making amends now.

The remembrance of your generosity and kindness will last many lifetimes.

Don't leave your family hurting, wishing things could have been different, and talking about you negatively later. Is there something you are hiding about yourself from others? Could there be some unspoken pain that, if brought out in the open, would help everyone understand why things are the way they are? Are there habits, past or present, which need to be addressed so there are no surprises after you're gone? Are you fearful about some things in your past that you really don't think God is big enough to handle? God's Word tells us that's just not true.

Even to your old age and gray hairs I am he, I am he who will sustain you. I have made you and I will carry you; I will sustain you and I will rescue you. (Isaiah 46:4)

I encourage you to leave this world with a clean slate. Tell it all, my friend. Tell it all. Tell the truth, the whole truth, and nothing but the truth. Make sure that no word can be said about you that is contrary to what everyone already knows, so your legacy will not be stained by something you left hidden during your life, which is discovered after you're gone.

Those conversations are hard, but they are essential to a legacy that is spotless and unblemished. They might begin like this:

- Your mother and I have something to tell you.
- I want you to know that I'm not perfect.
- There are some things in my life you don't know about.
- I don't want you to hear these things from anyone else.
- I've been to some places and done some things that you don't know about.
- There are some things in our family I want you to know about so they go no further.
- Knowing what I know may help you see things in a different light.
- I want you to know I haven't been totally honest with you.
- I didn't get to where I am without making some mistakes along the way.
- Poor choices haunted me earlier in life; I don't want you to make the same mistakes.

Clear the air, admit wrongdoings, ask for forgiveness, and strive to make your relationships right. Many fear that the admission of wrongdoing will ruin a legacy and stain a memory beyond repair. Quite the contrary. What you will do by admitting your mistakes and failures is to permit your family members to clean out theirs. Through this, you usher in a world of hope for your kids and freedom in your family. You lay the groundwork for mental, emotional, and spiritual health. They'll remember the fun times, but also your admission of wrongdoing will be burned in their hearts forever. Not in a way that taints their memory of you, but in a way that causes them to remember your strength of character. Funny, isn't it? The hope will be ushered into the lives of your children, not through your perfection, but through your imperfections.

They will remember you in the following ways:

- Remember when Dad shared about his life and let us know we, too, can make it?
- Remember when Mom admitted her problem with anger and let us know why that existed in her life?
- Remember when Dad told us the truth about our family?
- Remember when Mom shared with us how important it is not to hide anything?
- Remember when Dad cried and shared about his hurt and his poor choices?
- Remember when Mom told us what really happened?
- Remember when Mom and Dad gave us all hope and let us know that we're all going to be okay?

Go make memories before you lose yours. Leave a legacy of hope and influence.

CHAPTER 27

Transferring What You Believe to Be Important

Having so fond an affection for you, we were well pleased to impart to you not only the gospel of God but also our own lives, because you had become very dear to us.

1 Thessalonians 2:8 (NASB)

Most people don't know that in 1969, I was the Oklahoma Bible Quiz champ for memorizing hundreds of Scriptures as a ninth grader in Tulsa. I have always believed in hiding God's Word in my heart, for I know that out of the abundance of my heart, my mouth speaks (Luke 6:45, NKJV). In reflection, I think that Scripture memorization has been my way of expressing my love for God and commitment to Christ.

Others express themselves in various ways. Many preach. Some are great people of prayer. Some really get into worship. There are many diligent workers in the far and distant mission field sacrificially serving others. Some express their love for God through music as singers, choir members, or musicians. Some teach Bible studies, while others have gifts to create great devotionals and share deep biblical insights. Some serve on church boards or ministry committees. All have ways of expressing their love for God and their commitment to Him. It takes all kinds of kinds, doesn't it?

I believe my expression of love for God is through my knowledge of His Word and through the quieter actions of meeting the needs of people. That's the way I transfer what I believe to be important. I get involved, show up, and spend time in the company of those God has placed, for whatever reason, before me.

What's your expression of your faith? Whatever it is, I bet money the impact of your expression of your commitment to God can be seen no clearer than when you are fully present, engaging in discussions, and leading by example. This all takes place through the sharing of your life, in particular with your children.

The apostle Paul might call it his *with-ness*. No matter how Paul expressed himself to many, everyone who knew him would remember how he was with people. He visited, wrote to them, and spent time with them to share with them the true reflection of a man who was touched by the hand of God.

For me, it's all about presence.

Your Presence

And I was with you in weakness and in fear and much trembling.
(1 Corinthians 2:3, ESV)

I told you I recently attended the funeral of my dear friend, David. I also said I walked in after the service started. I knew I was going to be late, as flight schedules just weren't working in my favor. As soon as I landed in Indy, I got a call from David's daughter asking how long it would be before I arrived at the service. They even postponed the funeral thirty minutes awaiting my arrival.

When I arrived, I was ushered up front to sit with David's wife and two daughters. We exchanged hugs, shed tears, and held hands as we watched the celebration of a life well lived by our dear, dear loved one. We knew he had been ushered out of our presence and into the presence of God. Not much was said. Nothing needed to be spoken. Words would have been inadequate.

Sometimes we put too much value on words. We think what we have to say is so important. We wait so anxiously to speak our minds that we miss the greater truth that it is more about who we are than about those words that come out of our mouth. Or we miss opportunities to be there for someone because we don't know what to say. Or we're too afraid we'll say the wrong thing,

The message of presence is greatly underrated, while the effectiveness of a timely word that sounds good is significantly overrated.

so we avoid someone in need. Sadly, many are convinced that words trump the presence they might have in someone's life. The desire to avoid the awkwardness and embarrassment of being tongue-tied or speechless keeps people from simply giving the gift of their presence. Sometimes one's mere presence speaks volumes.

The message of presence is greatly underrated, while the effectiveness of a timely word that sounds good is significantly overrated. There are many situations where words don't and can't adequately convey a message of comfort, hope, or encouragement. Don't underestimate your presence in the life of your children. You are *speaking* louder than you know and your kids are observing more than you think.

I would suggest this to you as well. It's your presence in your teens' life that will give you the greatest opportunities to transfer the biblical concepts you long to share. You may have gifts that give you an opportunity to share your faith through a number of outlets, but none are as effective as your presence in the life of your children. Just show up. Then they can spend time with you and understand who you are, not just see what you do.

Your attendance at sporting events, special events, award ceremonies, and any other occasion to watch your children achieve something, sends a message of value to them. Your effort to be there sends an invitation of involvement that, hopefully, will one day bring a response from that wisdom-seeking child in need of counsel. When you demonstrate your *with-ness* to your children, they'll seek you out when they need trusted advice.

When you feel like just being present isn't working, you're probably not trusting that the seeds you sow into their lives will come to fruition. God promises to "complete that which He has started" (Philippians 1:6). It's your lack of patience in God's timing that can get in the way of His plan for your child. We all feel like *it's not working!* at times when we don't see the fruits of our labor in our kids. In those times, remember this Scripture, "Let us not become weary in doing good, for at the proper time we will reap a harvest if we do not give up" (Galatians 6:9). Between the time of planting seeds and the time of harvest, there is waiting and watching. It's a virtue called patience that helps parents understand and embrace the truth that sometimes you just have to let seeds grow in their own time.

During those growing times, remain patient and allow God to do His thing. If you're in your child's field always churning and turning up the soil, you might keep that harvest from happening. That's pretty hard for many parents who feel like they are limited in their time. Out of the goodness of their heart, they keep talking and talking and talking…because they don't see or hear the immediate response to their presence. Have patience, my friend. Your presence is noted and recognized.

After my friend David's funeral service and burial of this rock of a man, we all stood around in the Indiana sun, feeling uneasy as to when to say our goodbyes. David's wife, Amy, didn't mention one thing about anything I had shared. She didn't feel comfort or relief from her grief by any insights imparted by anyone. She did say this one thing as we all started to leave, "Thanks for being here, Mark." It was the greatest gift I could have given her and her daughters. Nothing needed to be said; words would have only ruined the message only presence could convey. The same goes for your attendance at the activities your children deem important. You're not there to do your thing; you're there to be involved in their thing.

Your Discussions

Your presence offers the invitation for discussion. Your discussions give an opportunity to engage your child, affirm the relationship, and open the door for future discussions. You don't have to come to a conclusion at the end of every discussion. I like to leave all of mine open-ended. That gives kids reason to come back and have more discussion.

This is what they want in discussions with you. They want wisdom, even if they don't know that's what they want. They are looking for a welcoming place where they can discuss what they think, even if it's pure craziness and counter to what you believe. They seek someone to listen and help them process what's floating around in their heads. They are looking for a safe place to share deep thoughts and hidden feelings. Remember, don't lecture. Your kids want to learn what they want to know, not what you want them to know. They want to be trained, not taught.

If you're asking yourself the question, *Well, if I can't lecture, then how do I engage in discussion?*, here are some pointers:

1. **Ask questions.** Show interest in what they have to say by asking them to go deeper into their thoughts and share from a more personal level. Questions convey value, your attentiveness, and it invites them to share their thoughts with you. Here's a few to get you started.

- Why do you think that way?
- Do you think your thoughts are in line with what you believe?
- What do your friends say about this topic?
- What do you think will be important in this matter ten years from now?
- Has something happened in your life that makes you feel this way?
- Have you always felt this way?

- Have you been afraid to share these thoughts with others?
- What do you think about…?

2. **Make comments that communicate that you are listening.** Say things or little comments that assure them you are tracking with them and hanging on every word. Those comments are short conversation affirmations to show you are focused on the responses of your teen. Here are some comments that I use.

- That's interesting; I never thought of it that way.
- Really?
- Wow!
- What led you to believe that?
- Do you struggle with what you're thinking?
- You're kidding me.
- That really happened?
- Then what did you say?
- How long ago did this happen?
- When did you start feeling this way?
- Are you doing okay in the midst of dealing with your feelings?

3. **Don't talk in long diatribes and sermons.** Talk in short bursts. Be prepared to ask many questions to keep the conversation going. When I interview kids on our radio program, I use this method to keep discussions moving along. When I initially ask a question, I take one word from their answer and put it into the form of the next question.

Here's an example of a conversation using this method.

Question: What's one of the biggest mistakes you made in the last month?

Answer: I **cheated** on a test.

Question: Why did you **cheat** on a test?

Answer: I thought I was going to **fail**.

Question: Why did you think you were going to **fail**?

Answer: I always **fail**.

Question: Why do you always **fail**?

Answer: School has always been **hard**.

Question: Why has school been **hard**?

Answer: People don't like me very much 'cause I'm **stupid**.

Question: Do you think you're **stupid**?

Answer: Yeah, I just **say** things that are impulsive.

Question: What kind of things do you **say**?

Answer: Mostly **mean** things.

Question: Why **mean** things?

Answer: Because most of my friends seem to be out to get me.

You can see how this conversation went from a mistake made in the past month to *my friends seem out to get me.* I call it fishing. I'm fishing for responses, and I really don't care what I catch. As long as I'm allowed to fish, I hope to cast the bait deeper and deeper and deeper, until they start sharing their hearts. In the above conversation, I went from asking about his behavior to diving into the issues of their heart. No lecture, just discussion.

4. **Don't repeat.** Remember how I said some parents have the tendency to tell you what they're going to tell you, then tell you, then tell you what they told you? This conversation style is rooted in the best of intentions, with a desire to pass on some good information. But saying things over and over again doesn't draw your kids to you. It pushes them away. Mom and Dad, say it one time and leave it alone. Bring it up in another discussion, but not in the same one twice.

Here's why I encourage you to limit your repetitiveness. If your children think they're going to hear the same thing over and over, they'll shut down, and all the wisdom you have to share (and which they greatly need) will never be heard. You won't be given a chance to break through to a child who is deeply in need.

5. **Don't talk just to fix your teen.** Men like to fix things. They don't want to hear the entire problem. They just want to hear what they need to do to fix it. Dad, beware. Your intent to fix your son may come across as challenging his manhood. You may unintentionally remind him that he doesn't have it all together. That's not a message any man desiring maturity wants to hear. Your intent to fix your daughter may just remind her she is broken, not exactly how a young lady wants to be seen.

Be careful in your discussions and deliberations. Know the importance of each, as these interactions help form your children's view of life and how it applies to their world. Formation of beliefs takes place through challenging discussion and counter discussion. So if a lecture is the only form of communication with your kids, future counter discussions won't happen. Don't plan discussions just to transfer what you believe. Let discussions develop over time that help them cultivate all the thoughts in their head. In the process, your beliefs will be conveyed. They will get interested in what you think when you get interested in what they think.

If you're wondering what to talk about, just watch the news one night or glance at a newspaper looking for things they heard about or are experiencing. These conversations can all begin with, "Hey, what do you think about..."

- homosexuality and the gender issue argument?
- the world of politics today?
- the legalization of marijuana?
- all the shootings in our country?
- the issue of people who are in this country illegally?
- why it's so hard to love the unlovely?

- the church you grew up in and what that means to you?
- thinking less of yourself?
- abortion and women's rights for equality?
- sex trafficking?

There's plenty to talk about if you remember you're not there for them to hear you. You are there to be able to listen to them.

Your Example

We did this...to offer ourselves as a model for you to imitate.
(2 Thessalonians 3:9)

I do things with my kids so I have an opportunity to speak into their lives. I want to show them what it means to flesh out not only a relationship with Christ, but also one with my wife, my kids, my friends, people I don't even know, those in authority, and those who are destitute. Perhaps the bigger reason is just to have fun together.

I don't set a goal during each time together of teaching them certain spiritual truths. The truths naturally come out as we engage in activities together. It's about helping them see examples of what all those teachings look like as they enter their teen years. They want examples. They want the word to become flesh and dwell among them. They want to see a living example of one who can apply timeless truth to the crazy culture they live in.

Your teen wants to see a living example of one who can apply timeless truth to the crazy culture they live in.

In your teens' world where worth and value are based on appearance and performance, they need to see and hear real substance. It is important for them not only to hear you transfer the values you hold dear into their Christian walk, but also to see what they look like in real life. As you walk and as you talk, as you sit down together and as you travel, they need to see how you act in different situations so they can imitate a lifestyle that is attractive and fulfilling. It's their desire to see Scripture lived out in someone's life with a spirit of humility and integrity. They want to see their parents respond with grace and strength when life deals you health issues, tragedy, great loss, or financial struggles. They long for that bigger perspective I've mentioned more than once.

Above all, they long for an example where people are truly known by the love they have for one another and where judgment is left to the Father. You're it! You were chosen before the world was created to be that example for these particular kids—your children. When you choose to fulfill this role in their lives, remember that the Christian life is more caught than taught. It's better shown than talked about.

This should be your goal in all you do: Be an example of one who lives life well within this contrary culture. Show them what Jesus looks like when they look at you. You have a presence in their lives and a legacy for them to remember because you had many, many discussions and your life was a good example in a crazy world.

You're not there to lead. You're there to give them someone to follow.

Final Thoughts

This contrary culture is tough. It's an atmosphere of challenging values, shallow relationships, and permissive alternatives in a culture that is more about expressing than listening. You and I have said we're glad that we don't have to grow up in a time like this. But your kids do. And if we don't make some changes in our ways to counter the effects this culture is having on our teens, I fear we will lose them relationally, spiritually, and emotionally.

My desire for you is that by going through these chapters, you have learned to love your teens better. You can give everything to your teens and not have love, and you both will have nothing. You can be the greatest in your profession and be known to millions for what you do, but if you don't have love in your home, all that recognition really doesn't stand for much. But if you keep deepening your relationship with your teens, then your children's children will remember you.

May the Lord bless you and your kids as you strive to seek to become the family that He has in mind for you. If you're ever in East Texas and want a great cup of coffee, come see us at Heartlight. The welcome mat is always out and coffee is always just a push button away.

Mark Gregston

About the Author

Mark Gregston is an author, speaker, radio host, and the founder of a residential counseling center for struggling teens located in Longview, Texas. Mark's passion for helping teens can be seen in his forty years of involvement with families as a youth pastor, Young Life area director, and now, as the Executive Director of Heartlight, where he has lived with and helped over three thousand teens.

His years of experience have prepared Mark to share his insights and wisdom about parenting pre-teens and adolescents. He does so through radio, seminars, books, parent retreats and conferences held around the country throughout the year.

Parenting Today's Teens with Mark Gregston radio program can be heard on over two thousand radio outlets. His best-selling books, all written to help parents understand and counter the effects of today's culture on their teens, are a must for every parent's library. And if some weekend Mark isn't home on the ranch in Texas, spending time with kids and families, he's traveling the country leading seminars or conferences, or speaking at various events.

Mark's relational mindset, coupled with his wit and humor, entertains moms and dads with practical advice for avoiding chaos, implementing change, and handling difficult situations with their teens. Mark's message resonates with parents of all ages.

He has been married to his high school sweetheart, Jan, for forty-three years, and has two kids and four grandkids. He lives in Longview, Texas with the Heartlight staff, sixty high school kids, twenty-five horses, his dog, Stitch, one llama, and a prized donkey named Toy.

For more information, visit:
www.HeartlightMinistries.org
www.ParentingTodaysTeens.org

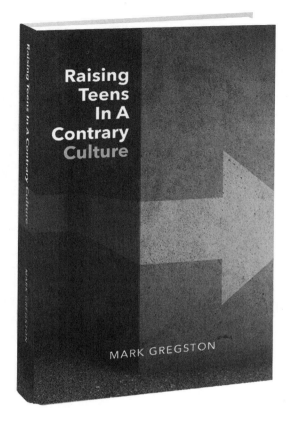

To order more copies of

Raising Teens
In A Contrary Culture

Order online at:

- www.HeartlightMinistries.org/resources
- or call 1-866-700-FAMILY (3264)

*Also available on Amazon.com and
ChristianBook.com*

WHEN IT COMES TO CRISIS, **THREE DAYS CAN CHANGE EVERYTHING.**

Are you in the middle of a family crisis? Know a family that is?
Our Families in Crisis Conference offers hope for a better future.
This three-day conference is taught and hosted by Mark Gregston,
Founder and Executive Director of Heartlight Ministries and host of
Parenting Today's Teens. Parents who attend will leave with a more
complete understanding of how to influence real change and help
lost teens find their way back on track.

The event is held on the beautiful Heartlight campus,
about 150 miles east of Dallas, Texas. **To learn more and register
visit FamiliesInCrisisConference.com or call 903.668.2173.**

Offering **help** and **hope**
to parents and teens
in a broken world.

For nearly 30 years we've provided a safe haven for positive change. Our 9–12 month residential counseling program offers struggling teens a relational atmosphere to develop healthier patterns during their most troubling times. We've fully invested in our campus facilities in East Texas as well as a caring staff, to more successfully create lasting change in the lives of teens.

For more information about admissions, please visit heartlightministries.org, call 903-668-2173.

♡ heartlight

Small group sunday school series that helps parents and grandparents with today's teens.

MIDDLE SCHOOL

Tough Guys and Drama Queens - A 9-week video course is a must for any parent of middle schoolers and homeschoolers as this series is packed with wisdom and gives parents a vision of what they could be in the life of their teens, helping all viewers understand today's teen culture. Mark shares what "works" and what "doesn't" and shares throughout new tried and true ways to successfully engage with your little tough guy or drama queen.

HIGH SCHOOL

Raising Teens in a Contrary Culture - This 9 lesson curriculum series is perfect for small groups, classes, community groups or groups of parents desiring to understand how to pursue the heart of their teen in an opposing culture that doesn't always support and back a parent's desire to raise godly teens in a confusing culture.

GRANDPARENTS

Leaving a Legacy of Hope - Grandparents have the opportunity to leave a legacy that will not soon be forgotten. For it is parents that influence, but it is grandparents who leave a legacy that offers hope and encouragement long after they're gone. A legacy is not just what you leave in your grandchild's bank account, but is measured by what you have deposited in their heart. This 8-week video series is a must for any grandparent.

To order, visit **www.ParentingTeenResources.org** or call **1-866-700-FAMILY (3264)**